Insurance: Concepts & Coverage

PROPERTY, LIABILITY, LIFE,
HEALTH AND RISK MANAGEMENT

by Marshall Wilson Reavis III, PhD

Published by:

FriesenPress

Suite 300 – 852 Fort Street
Victoria, BC, Canada V8W 1H8

www.friesenpress.com

Distributed to the trade by The Ingram Book Company

Table Of Contents

PREFACE

Insurance is a method by which individuals, families and organizations can be protected from financial loss that results from an unexpected or accidental happening. There are two basic types of insurance programs — personal insurance and commercial insurance. The major lines of insurance are Property, Liability, Life and Health.

In this book the primary features of the insurance policies will be explored to give the reader an understanding of the working of an insurance company and an insurance policy.

In the area of Personal Insurance the keystone of property insurance is the Homeowners Program which provides coverage for real and personal property as well as personal liability exposures.

The other major player in Personal Insurance is the Personal Automobile policy which provides protection for the user of the vehicle who may be held responsible for an accident. It also covers physical damage to the vehicle and provides medical expense insurance for its insureds and passengers.

Commercial Insurance is largely covered by the Commercial Package Policy (CPP) which is designed to meet the various coverage needs of commercial, industrial and mercantile businesses through its various policy forms. Available through the CPP program are policy forms for Commercial Property, Liability, Auto, Crime, Equipment Breakdown, and Inland and Ocean Marine insurance.

Workers Compensation and Employers Liability insurance will also be reviewed as it is a primary insurance coverage for businesses and other organizations. In addition to the noted coverages there will be other insurance programs and policies discussed in the book including an examination of a Risk Management Program.

We hope you will find this book to be of great value to you as insurance in its many forms is an economic necessity that affects your personal and business finances.

Marshall Wilson Reavis III, PhD

Insurance Education Publishers, LLC.

CHAPTER ONE

BASIC PRINCIPLES & CONCEPTS OF INSURANCE & THE INSURANCE INDUSTRY

INTRODUCTION.

During an introductory study, one finds that the insurance industry is many things to many people. It is a major financial institution which has great effect upon the economy of the country because of the large number of dollars that are paid in by policyholders which must be invested until it is time to pay claims.

It is also a large employer since there are thousands of insurance companies that employ or service the hundreds of thousands of agents and company representatives throughout the country and the world.

Finally, it is a social device since it serves to finance the rebuilding of properties after a loss, makes funds available for a child's education, builds estates for the beneficiaries of policyholders, pays for needed health care, protects the individual from financial loss in the event of an accident and assures lenders that if a mortgaged property is lost or destroyed the repayment of the loan will still be made.

Insurance is many things to many people. What will insurance be to you? The following sections discuss some basic principles and concepts which are important to an introductory study of the insurance industry. In many cases the insurance industry uses a language of its own. In studying the insurance industry it is important to understand these terms and concepts. The following material will aid you to understand the insurance industry, its products and its people.

WHAT IS INSURANCE?

By definition insurance is "a method by which interested members of a society can band together and collect funds to pay losses suffered later by members of the group."

There are other definitions of insurance available, some are related to its legal aspects, others to its economic importance and still others to its social effects. However, for the purpose of this book the definition given above is sufficient.

There are many stories as to when, where and how insurance began. One of some interest concerns the primitive Caveman who faced the possibility of loss of their goods and belongings at the hands of enemies and animals. The Cavemen found that when they left their caves for an extended hunting trip, upon their return, they would sometimes discover that one of the members' caves had been stripped of its belongings probably by animals or an enemy.

Finally a wise Caveman suggested that each put part of his own goods into the cave of each of the others. Then the Caveman said, if one cave is raided and all of its contents lost, all of the members would lose part of their goods, but none would lose all of their goods.

Thus, the concept of insurance was introduced—to spread risk among many so that no single member would lose everything.

Insurance has developed throughout the world in its commercial form for over 300 years. The insurance industry in the United States dates from the time of the Revolutionary War. Today there are over four thousand property and liability insurance companies and over two thousand life insurance companies operating in this country.

WHAT IS RISK?

Another term that is commonly used in the insurance industry is Risk. A generally accepted definition of risk is "uncertainty as to loss."

This definition of risk as used in insurance indicates that while it can be assumed that some individual will suffer a loss, there is uncertainty as to which individual will be affected in any given circumstance and at what time.

Insurance is often accused of being a form of gambling. However, there is an important difference. The concept of risk and uncertainty plays an important part in this difference.

One important factor which involves insurance is that there must be a certainty of loss with a certainty of no gain. This is interpreted to mean that the expense of the premium has become a certain loss while the no gain means that only as much as has been lost will be repaired, replaced or have its actual cash value paid.

Therefore one may lose but one may never gain from the insurance industry's product. This concept is what removes insurance from the area of gambling. In gambling there is both a chance of loss and a chance of gain.

WHAT MAKES A RISK INSURABLE?

It is generally accepted that there are four criteria or requirements which must be fulfilled in order that a risk can be considered to be insurable. These four are:

It must be one of a large homogeneous group. — This means that there are a large number of similar units which are exposed to loss in a relatively similar fashion and as a result, the law of large numbers can operate. This law allows the statistical process called probability to be applied in determining the probable number of losses that will occur and the amount of premium needed for the insurance program.

Any loss must be measurable in dollars and cents. — Since this is an economic loss, there must be a money value which can be established on the goods and services involved in the potential loss.

Not subject to catastrophic loss. — To be insurable, there has to be an element of an accidental happening to one of the many units exposed. If all the items to be considered were subject to a catastrophic loss; i.e., all located in the path of a weakened dam, then the factors of chance and probable loss could not apply. When they cannot apply, then the risk would not be insurable.

The loss must be a fortuitous (accidental) happening. — Intentional acts by a responsible party cannot be insured because they would conflict with the projections of uncertainty and probability. There must always be uncertainty as to which unit may be lost.

WHAT ARE A LOSS EXPOSURE, LOSS AND CLAIM?

There are three related concepts that are important to the study of insurance. These are loss exposure, loss and claim.

Loss Exposure. — Something or someone that can experience damage, destruction, disappearance, death, disability or illness because of the action of another person or of an accidental happening. Most loss exposures are insurable.

Loss. — The unintentional and unexpected reduction in economic value experienced by an individual or object due to the action of another or some accidental happening causing injury or damage.

Claim. — The demand made upon another party for recovery by a party that has suffered a loss. The action may be made against an individual, a firm, an organization or an insurance company.

WHAT IS A CAUSE OF LOSS?

A major term used in insurance is Cause of Loss (also called a Peril). Insurance coverage responds when a loss results from a cause of loss identifed in an insurance contract.

Examples of causes of loss are fire, windstorm, operation of a motor vehicle, burglary, acts of negligence, accident and sickness and other conditions that can cause a loss. Sometimes the cause of loss is called an Act of God, particularly when it is an unusual and unexpected, perhaps even a catastrophic happening.

WHAT IS A HAZARD?

A Hazard is a condition which feeds a cause of loss (peril). There are four types of hazards which contribute to the loss caused by perils that are covered under an insurance policy. These are physical, moral, morale and legal hazards.

Physical Hazards. — These include such things as a broken stair step, trash which has collected, weeds near a building, worn tires on a motor vehicle, the lack of a burglar alarm or inadequate fire protection equipment.

Moral Hazards. — Those things that deal with dishonest intent or exposure to dishonest persons. For example, embezzlement or arson are moral hazards.

Morale Hazards. — These deal with the area of indifference or laziness. Such as an employee smoking where prohibited, removing guards from machinery, not wearing safety equipment or leaving doors unlocked.

Legal Hazards. — Conditions brought about by statute, judicial decision or administrative regulation which create a potential loss exposure that had not existed before are legal hazards. For example, a government agency rules that a particular product may cause cancer and should be removed from the marketplace. A firm that manufactures such a product could become the object of lawsuits arising out of the use of its product because of the new regulation.

WHAT IS INDEMNITY?

An insurance policy may state that it will indemnify the insured in the event of a loss. Indemnity means that the insurance company will pay the insured the money value of the loss.

Under a property policy this means that the insurance company will repair or replace or pay the insured the "actual cash value" of the item or property lost or destroyed. The insured when indemnified, will receive no more than the value of the property at the time of loss. Actual Cash Value is defined as the Replacement Cost (at the time of loss) minus Depreciation (the reduction in value due to wear, use or obsolescence).

Liability policies are also policies of indemnity. However, they state that the policy will pay on behalf of the insured. Under these policies the insurance company does not repay the insured for value lost, but instead pays the injured party such monies as the insured is required to pay because of a loss caused by the insured.

WHAT IS INSURABLE INTEREST?

Another important concept in insurance is Insurable Interest. This has to do with who or what may be insured and by whom. Insurable interest exists if the party purchasing the policy would suffer economic loss if the person or item insured were to die or be damaged, destroyed, lost or cause damage to another person or object.

In all types of insurance one party must have such an insurable interest before a contract of insurance can be purchased on or for another party. With Life insurance the insurable interest must exist at the time the policy is written, while the relationship need not have to continue until the death of the insured.

However in Property and Liability insurance there also must be an insurable interest at the time of loss as well as when the policy is issued. For example in Property insurance, the relationship of values between a mortgagee and mortgagor must be determined at the time of loss. This is because the values may differ from the amount that they were at the time the policy was issued.

WHO ARE THE PARTIES TO THE INSURANCE CONTRACT?

With a Property insurance policy the contract parties are the Insured and the Insurance Company. Under a Liability insurance contract the parties are the Insured, the Insurance Company and the "Third-Party" Claimant.

In Life insurance the parties are the Insured, the Owner, the Beneficiary and the Insurance Company. Health insurance contract parties are the Insurance Company and the Insured participants.

HOW IS INSURANCE MARKETED?

There are various types of insurance companies as well as several methods of marketing their products. The companies are generally classified by the type of corporate structure under which they operate. There are also several types of government insurance operations.

Private insurance companies. The major forms of property and liability insurance companies are stock companies, mutual companies and reciprocal insurance exchanges. These companies have a home office in a single state but often operate in other states as authorized by those states.

Stock insurance companies. — These are corporations chartered by a state to conduct an insurance business. To start the business, individuals buy shares and these funds are used to form the corporation. The invested capital is used to fund the insurance company's operations until the organization generates enough business to pay operating costs out of current income. The paid-in capital also serves as the surplus fund guaranteeing the fulfillment of policy obligations during the early days of the organization.

The characteristics of a stock insurance company are: paid-in capital appears in its financial statement, the board of directors is elected by the stockholders and some portion of earnings may be paid to stockholders as dividends on their stock.

Mutual insurance companies. — Such organizations are owned by their policyholders. Before they can receive authority to operate they must meet a statutory requirement on the amount of premium and number of policies that it can immediately issue upon authorization. This requirement makes it difficult to start a mutual insurance company today.

A mutual insurance company may be identified as different from a stock insurance company by the following factors: there is no capital stock outstanding, the members of the board of directors are elected by the policyholders as there are no stockholders and the funds remaining after paying all costs of operations (including additions to all surplus and contingency funds) are distributed to the policyholders as policy dividends.

Reciprocal insurance exchange. — These firms are sometimes called an inter-insurance exchange. They are similar to a mutual insurance company as they are owned by their members. The policyholders, called subscribers, establish an exchange and insure one another. They also contract with an attorney-in-fact to operate the exchange under the control of an advisory board.

Each policyholder is both an insured and an insurer since the contracts are exchanged on a reciprocal basis. A premium called a deposit is paid in advance. Dividends may be paid to the subscribers based on operating results.

Public insurance companies. There are insurance programs that are underwritten by both the federal government as well as state governments. Some of these programs are voluntary while others are compulsory.

Voluntary programs include federal programs for the military, crops, financial institution deposits, security dealer transactions, crime and mortgage insurance. State government programs include life, title, automobile, medical malpractice and workers compensation insurance.

Compulsory insurance programs include federal Social Security plans for retirement, survivors, disability and health coverage. In six states, workers compensation insurance is only available from a state fund. Unemployment benefits are provided through state programs, although funding comes from employers and the federal government. Non-occupational health insurance is mandatory in several states and Puerto Rico.

WHO ARE THE INSURANCE PRODUCERS?

The marketing arm of the insurance company is the insurance producer. Yet the approach to marketing by insurance companies varies. Some may use more than one approach while others use only one. To review these various methods consider the following as the "A, B, C, D, E, S" of insurance marketing. While many states now issue a single "Producer" license, which encompasses both agents and brokers, all the methods of marketing mentioned above are discussed here.

Agents. — This is the traditional way of marketing all types of insurance. Under the American Agency System which developed in the early years of the insurance industry the agent is an independent business owner. As an agent the producer represents the insurance company in the sales transactions and must live up to the terms an agency contract with the insurance company. An agent generally will represent several insurance companies and "owns" the renewal right to the policies written for clients.

Brokers. — The technical difference between a broker and an agent is that the broker represents the client (insured) while the agent represents the insurance company at the time the transaction is made. It is the broker's function to search among the various insurance companies to find the best possible combination of coverages at the most reasonable price for the client. A broker must place the insurance contract through an authorized agent of the insurance company selected. The broker is also an independent contractor who controls the renewals of the contracts obtained for clients.

Commercial producers. — This is the large multi-office organization which operates throughout the United States and in some cases is multi-national in scope. Often they are large organizations whose stock is sold publicly. Their clients are generally large businesses and organizations. The commercial producer provides expertise in all major insurance related operations (loss control, claims, underwriting) and may serve as a consulting risk manager.

Direct writers. — This system of marketing insurance involves employees who are the sales force for an insurance organization. The method of compensation may be salary, commission or both. They can only sell their company's product. Another form of direct selling is "mass merchandising" which involves the solicitation of certain lines of insurance by mail, telephone or various media. Under this approach the prospect submits the application and receives the policy without ever meeting with the producer.

Exclusive representatives. — This is a system similar to the direct writer. The difference is that they must first offer the business to their insurance company but if it is rejected, they may place it with another company.

Surplus and Excess Lines producers. — When a producer cannot find a market for a client's insurance with an insurance company admitted to do business in the state, a non-admitted insurance company may be used. However, this requires a specific license and the producer must meet other state regulatory requirements such as paying premium taxes in order to use a non-admitted insurance company.

HOW ARE INSURANCE COMPANIES REGULATED?

Insurance policies, companies and producers are regulated by the various states "in the public interest." An individual state can regulate how an insurance company may write a particular class of business, a certain form of policy and the rate and premium that can be used.

The states have Insurance Departments that are headed by an Insurance Commissioner or Director who oversees the insurance business of the state. This includes the licensing of insurance companies and producers as well as overseeing the financial well being of the insurance companies operating in the state.

The federal government is also involved in regulation of some phases of insurance particularly health insurance coverages where the government mandates that insurance companies provide specific coverages on their policies.

CONSIDER THE ORGANIZATION OF AN INSURANCE COMPANY.

In order to provide for the protection from economic loss to individuals, business firms and other organizations the insurance companies have developed a basic operational format.

This format provides for three major functions: Underwriting, Marketing and Claims. In addition there are other activities which must be performed in order to serve policyholders. These others can be grouped into a fourth functional area called Administration.

Underwriting. — An underwriting department selects from the applicants for insurance those who meet its underwriting requirements. The areas of underwriting involved depend on the lines of insurance the insurance company is eligible to underwrite based on its "Certificate of Authority" as issued by the various states.

A property and liability insurance company can issue either monoline or multiple peril policies. An example of the first type would be a workers compensation policy and the latter a homeowners policy. Personal life and health insurance can be monoline or group policies.

Since there are many types of insurance policies and lines of coverage, an individual underwriter may specialize in one particular area of interest or become a generalist handling several types of policies. This often depends upon the size of the insurance company and the types of policies that it underwrites. Property and liability insurance companies may divide their underwriting departments into Commercial and Personal lines. Life insurance and health insurance companies may have a department for individual insurance policies and one for group policies.

Within an Underwriting department, others who may assist in the underwriting function are actuaries, loss control personnel, medical and research staff.

Marketing. — The primary role of the marketing department is to make the public aware of the various lines of insurance products available from the insurance company. There are several methods of marketing insurance that are used. Some insurance companies may use more than one approach depending on circumstances such as geographic territory and state regulation.

The insurance company marketing efforts may be centralized in the home office or they may use regional and/or branch offices as the distribution system. The marketing department will often have a field staff that calls on or supervises the efforts of those making sales to the public.

To support the marketing efforts there are related tasks within an insurance company including advertising, public relations, publications, sales and technical training and new product development.

Claims. — One well known insurance executive has said "We must always remember that we in the insurance industry are in the business of paying claims."

This is a good concept to remember for it is because of the concern that they may suffer some type of economic loss that causes individuals and firms to purchase insurance. Thus when a loss occurs, the insurance company must make every effort to process and pay a just claim as promptly as possible.

The organization of the claim department varies depending on the type of insurance written. For property and liability insurance, there are both claims representatives that work inside the office and those who work outside in the field.

The outside claims person visits the scene of a loss, investigates, interviews witnesses, evaluates the loss, negotiates and makes settlements with insureds and claimants. In the event of litigation, the claims adjuster may work with the defense attorney handling the case.

In the life and health insurance industry claims are processed in the office based on the provisions of the policy. This may require review of the policy application and prior medical records of the insured. Contested claims may result in litigation which is handled by the claims staff along with defense attorneys.

Supervising the claims activities are senior claims persons who have many years of experience and may have medical and/or law degrees. Others involved in the claim process are attorneys, appraisers, claim auditors, loss analysts and medical staff.

Administration. — The last functional group Administration will vary among insurance companies depending on their size, the type of insurance written and other factors. For example, all insurance companies will have some accounting and investment activities and an IT function.

Other administrative areas include human relations, education and training, purchasing, library, food service, document reproduction, communications, transportation and dozens of other activities needed to maintain a modern day insurance company.

With some companies these services span not only a home office, but branch offices throughout the country and in some cases the world.

Obviously there is almost any type of job in an insurance company that might be found in the administration of any other commercial or industrial firm. Insurance is an ever growing and important industry in this country and throughout the world.

THE INSURANCE CONTRACT.

Another basic concept of insurance that is necessary to understand is that of the insurance policy which is a form of contract. Therefore it is important to first understand the elements of a contract and then to review the parts of an insurance policy. Also included is some information on special characteristics of contracts.

Elements of a Contract. — There are four basic elements of a contract. Each of these four elements must be present in a contract or it is not legally binding. These are the offer and acceptance, consideration, legal object and competent parties.

Offer and Acceptance (Agreement). — Under the law of contracts one party makes an offer and the other accepts the offer as a part of making a contract. This is called the agreement. Sometimes when the first party makes an offer, the second party will not accept it but makes a counter-offer. The first party can then accept the counter-offer or reject it and propose another counter-offer. Eventually this requirement of a contract will be fulfilled.

Consideration. - For a contract to be binding there must be some form of consideration (something of value) given in exchange by the buyer to the seller. Money is the most common form of consideration given.

Legal Object. — The object of a contract must be legal for trade before a contract is enforceable. In other words if two parties agree to an illegal transaction and one party fails to live up to the agreement, the second party could not receive help from the courts to enforce the contract since the transaction was illegal.

Competent Parties. — The parties involved in making a contract must be competent. There are two types of incompetent parties. The first includes minors who have not reached the age of majority and who are legally called infants. The second type of incompetent is the individual who has been judged mentally deminished by a court.

Generally contracts are not enforceable if made by minors or by those who do not have their mental faculties at the time the contract is formed. With minors there may be some exceptions with respect to necessities such as food, clothing and shelter.

Parts of an Insurance Contract. — There are five basic parts to an insurance policy. The first four are referred to as the "D-I-C-E" provisions. They are the following:

Declarations. — This component personalizes the policy to a given insured or insureds. The purpose of the declaration page is to state certain facts about the parties and the contract. It contains the necessary information to identify the insured(s), the exposure to be covered, the insurance limits and coverages provided, the rates and premiums charged, the inception and expiration dates and times for the coverage, the policy number and the name of the insurance agent and insurance company.

Insuring agreement. — This is a statement in broad general terms of the coverage being provided in the policy by the insurance company. The insuring agreement is then tempered by the provisions, conditions and exclusions within the policy.

Conditions. — Because an insurance policy is a legal contract, it is necessary to spell out the rights, duties and responsibilities of the parties involved. The conditions are the vehicle used for that purpose. A condition affecting coverage may be found in any part of an insurance contract.

Exclusions. — The exclusions limit the coverage granted by the insuring agreement to the scope intended by the insurance company for the particular policy form. It may appear to be unusual to first grant and then take away coverage to arrive at the desired specific insurance. However to spell out each kind of loss covered would be voluminous. Consequently the insurance agreement is covered in one section and the exclusions in another. It should be noted that exclusions affecting coverage may be found in any part of the contact.

Endorsements. — These are the fifth part of an insurance contract. Endorsements are attachments which can be added to a policy to amplify the wording or change its meaning or to add or restrict coverage. They are used to adapt the policy to the needs of an individual insured. In life and health insurance the endorsement form is called a "rider".

Special Characteristics of Contracts. — There are a number of special legal characteristics of contracts which are not unique to insurance contracts. However they do aid in explaining some of the basic concepts upon which insurance policies are based. These are the following:

Aleatory contracts. — When equal value is not paid by both parties to a contract it becomes an aleatory contract. For example an insured pays a $400 annual premium for a $100,000 property insurance policy covering a dwelling. If there is a loss, the insurance company will pay up to $100,000.

Contract of adhesion. — This is a contract prepared by one party which must be accepted "as is" by the other party. There is no barter for conditions under such a contract. The lesser party "adheres" to the terms offered. Courts generally resolve any ambiguity in the contract in favor of the accepting party.

Conditioned contract. — This is a contract that is subject to conditions precedent or in the future before it can be completed. For example an insurance policy which is issued "in consideration of the premium having been paid" it does promise to pay in the future if necessary in order to complete the contract.

Executory contract. — This is a contract that promises action (to be executed) at some later date. An insurance company promises to pay when a loss occurs at some later time.

Unilateral contract. — When only one party to a contract makes a promise that is enforceable the contract is "unilateral." The insured pays a premium to the insurance company that promises to pay a loss if it occurs. That act, the payment of the loss, is enforceable.

Good Faith and Fair Dealing. — An insurance contract must be entered into by both parties in good faith and with fair dealing. This means that both parties to the contract can expect that the information provided is accurate and can be relied upon. From contract law there are some terms that reflect this expectation and the consequences of failing to do so in the insurance transaction.

Contract of utmost good faith. — Partly because the insurance contract is aleatory, the parties enter into an agreement where mutual faith is of paramount importance. The legal principle of "uberrimae fiedei" (utmost good faith) has historical significance to the insurance transaction. Any information about the risk known by one party should be known to the other. Courts have given meaning to the principle of utmost good faith through the doctrines of misrepresentation, warranty and concealment.

Misrepresentation. — A representation is an oral or written statement made by the applicant prior to or at the time of the contract. It involves an inducement for the insurance company to issue the policy. If this information is false it is a misrepresentation and may be grounds to void the coverage if the information was material to the issuance of the contract.

Warranty. — This is a promise made by the applicant that is made part of the contract. For example the insured agrees to always have a working burglar alarm whenever the premises are closed for business. Failure to do so is a breach of the warranty and can be grounds to void the policy.

Concealment. — This is an intentional act by an applicant to fail to disclose material facts about the risk to be insured. Such an act can be grounds to void the contract.

CHAPTER TWO
BASIC PRINCIPLES & CONCEPTS OF PROPERTY INSURANCE

INTRODUCTION.

Property may be defined as anything that can be reduced to exclusive possession. It can be tangible (land, structures and household goods) or intangible (the right to use and enjoy tangible property) and it can be real or personal.

When property is damaged, destroyed or disappears, there is financial loss because of the reduced value of the property (direct loss) or from the loss of the use of the property (indirect loss).

The most common personal policy for the property loss exposure is the Homeowners policy. Most commercial property is insured under the Commercial Property Part of the Commercial Package Policy (CPP) or it can be issued as a monoline policy.

TYPES AND CHARACTERISTICS OF PROPERTY.

Property may be classified as either real or personal. The characteristics of these types of property are factors which are important in reviewing property insurance.

Real property. — The two types of real property are unimproved land and improved land (structures attached). The interest of individuals in improvements to land is also considered real property.

Unimproved land. — Is real estate that has no permanent improvements. The value of land may be determined by how it can be used. For example, it may contain valuable resources such as water, minerals, tillable soil, timber or wildlife. There also may be commercial value in the natural attraction of land such as caves, lakes or trails. Land value can be reduced by erosion, flood, earthquake, fire or regulation.

Improved land. — This is real property with something added of permanent value such as a structure. In addition to buildings other types of structures include in-ground swimming pools, lawn sprinkler systems, piping or wiring, septic tanks, wells and piers.

While land both improved and unimproved has value the land itself is seldom insured. However, the right to ownership of land may be insured. For example, a person holding an interest in real property can obtain Title insurance to protect against economic loss in the event the title is defective.

Title insurance will not guarantee the owner's right to retain possession of the property but will indemnify for loss that is within the scope of the title insurance. Examples are liens, encumbrances or forged deeds.

The type of structures and their use are the major features of real property to be considered in understanding property insurance. Structures may be made from a variety of materials and the use can be personal or commercial. In the sections that follow the Homeowners Program and the Commercial Property Insurance Form will be reviewed.

Dwellings. — Structures affixed to improved land. A dwelling is commonly considered a single family residence on its own plot of land. Not only is the living space considered real property but also excavations, foundations, underground piping, and plumbing systems. There are other types of dwellings equally distinctive including:

Dwellings rented to others. — Which is any type of dwelling that can be leased or rented with or without an option to buy.

Farm dwellings. — A one-to-four-family dwelling situated on individual or corporate owned property used for farming or ranching.

Personal Property. — All property other than real property is considered personal property and can be either tangible or intangible. It may also be owned or simply in one's possession.

Tangible personal property. — This includes that which a person may physically possess (furniture, clothing).

Intangible personal property. — Things which are possessed by a person yet are neither physical in nature nor capable of being touched (the promise made by an insurance policy, a copyright).

Types of Personal Property. — There are some types of personal property that can be considered part of the dwelling under certain circumstances. Examples include the following.

Fixtures. — Personal property once installed or attached may become part of the land or dwelling. This may be subject to local ordinance or statute. For example, the kitchen range is considered part of the dwelling in some jurisdictions but as personal property in others. A built-in oven would be considered part of the building in most cases.

Improvements and betterments. — These are alterations to real property made by a tenant which become part of the structure. The tenant has a right of use of these for the term of the lease. When the tenant leaves the Improvement and Betterments remain and become property of the owner.

Owned property. — An individual obtains the exclusive right to the property, its use and enjoyment, the right to transfer by sale and the obligation to pay any debt on the property. Ownership is the highest right an individual can possess in property.

Nonowned property. — Property that is held in a person's possession but is not owned involves a bailment. When an individual lends property to another, the owner is the bailor and the one receiving the property is the bailee.

A bailment has three elements: 1) Transfer of personal property possession without transfer of title, 2) Acceptance of possession by the bailee, 3) Expressed or implied agreement of the bailee to return the property to the bailor or to a person designated by the bailor.

The type of bailment determines the amount of care to be exercised by the bailee. When it is a bailment for the benefit of the bailor, the bailee possesses the property gratuitously and must only use prudent care.

If the bailment is for the sole benefit of the bailee, an extraordinary degree of care is required. Finally when the bailment is for the mutual benefit of the parties, the bailee is required to exercise ordinary care of a prudent person in similar circumstances.

UNDERWRITING PROPERTY INSURANCE.

Underwriting management of an insurance company establishes guidelines which cover the types of policies, procedures and exposures that an underwriter uses in selecting insureds. While there are many such guidelines the following illustrate the type of concerns faced by an underwriter in that selection decision.

In the review of an application for property insurance there are some standard areas which are considered. These can be identified by the acronym "C-O-P-E" which stands for Construction (wood, brick, masonry,

---

non-combustible), Occupancy (single, multi-tenant, manufacturing, retail), Protection (fire, theft, public, private), and Exposure (neighborhood, woods, water, other properties). These four areas, when approved, are of considerable assistance to the underwriting process.

CATEGORIES OF PROPERTY LOSS.

The two general categories of loss are 1) Direct loss — which causes a reduction in value of the property because it was destroyed, damaged or disappeared and 2) Indirect loss — which involves the consequences associated with the loss of use of the property such as additional living expense, loss of fair rental value, loss of rents, loss of use of additions and loss of income alterations.

PROPERTY CAUSES OF LOSS (PERILS).

Property insurance policies provide benefits based on losses that are caused by an event covered under the terms of the policy contract. These events are called "Causes of Loss" or "Perils" and are identified in the policy itself. Both tangible and intangible properties are exposed to a variety of perils.

There are three standard property causes of loss or perils forms. The "Causes of Loss — Basic Form" includes the perils of fire, lightning, windstorm, hail, riot or civil commotion, damage by aircraft or vehicles, smoke, explosion, vandalism, volcanic action, sinkhole collapse and sprinkler leakage. These are also referred to as "Named Perils."

The next level of property causes of loss is the "Causes of Loss — Broad Form". The Broad form includes all of the named perils found in the Basic form as well as the following perils: falling objects, weight of snow, ice or sleet, and water damage (accidental discharge or leakage of water or steam as a result of breaking apart or cracking of a domestic system or appliance).

The third and most liberal is the "Causes of Loss — Special Form" which provides what used to be called the "all-risks" coverage. This form covers any accidental cause of loss unless it is specifically excluded in the form.

On most property insurance forms Flood and Earthquake perils are excluded because of their catastrophic exposure. However they can be available in separate policies or by endorsement. There is an "Earthquake" Cause of Loss form available when the coverage is to be added to a commercial policy.

PROPERTY LOSS SETTLEMENT FEATURES.

Building and personal property insurance policies can be written on a replacement cost basis (RC), which provides "new for old" in the event of loss. Otherwise these policies are issued on an actual cash value basis (ACV) that deducts depreciation from the loss payment.

The financial loss is limited to the value of the property plus any income loss or extra expense. Insurance is the major technique to be used by individuals and families for protection from loss. However, loss control methods which involve both loss prevention and loss reduction activities are important for an insured in reducing the chance of loss.

Retention of risk in the form of a deductible is used with most insurance policies when dealing with property loss exposures. The use of a deductible also will tend to reduce premium costs.

A concurrent cause of loss occurs when more than one peril is involved in a loss. If one of the involved perils is excluded from coverage when concurrent causation occurs, and the other is covered, there may be problems in the settlement of the loss.

HOMEOWNERS PROGRAM.

The insurance approach used by most individuals and families to protect themselves from the financial consequences of loss to real and personal property is the Homeowners Program.

This program is available for those who own or rent a house, condominium or apartment and/or reside within such a unit. The dwelling must be used primarily as a residence, although some incidental occupancy is permitted such as a home office or studio.

Eligible groups for the program are: 1) Owner/occupants of private homes (one or two family dwellings, some insurance companies will cover up to four family dwellings), 2) Tenants of apartments, homes, mobile homes or condominiums and 3) Owner/occupants of condominium units.

The Dwelling Insurance program is available for those parties not eligible for a homeowners policy. There are also Mobile Home insurance policies for individuals and families in manufactured housing.

Under the Homeowners program the insured is defined as "the person named in the declarations as the insured, relatives who reside in the named insured's household and other persons under the age of twenty-one and in the care of the insured or a resident relative."

The Homeowners contract is called a package policy because it contains both property insurance and liability insurance in a single policy. The policy consists of the following parts:

Declarations — Information on who, what, where and when.

Insuring Agreement — A broad general statement of coverage provided.

Definitions — Terms and provisions found in the policy

Section I — Property Coverages

    Coverage A—Dwelling

    Coverage B—Other Structures

    Coverage C—Personal Property

    Coverage D—Loss of Use

Section II — Liability Coverages

    Coverage E—Personal Liability

    Coverage F—Medical Payments to Others

Conditions

Exclusions

Endorsements (if used)

Coverage A — Establishes the amount of insurance protection for the dwelling based on the replacement cost for the structure. The dwelling limit value selected provides the base from which the other three Section I coverages are determined.

Coverage B — Provides coverage for other structures (outbuildings) on the premises and is an additional dollar amount of insurance equal to ten percent of the amount selected for Coverage A.

Coverage C — Is the coverage for personal property of the insured. It is an additional dollar amount of insurance coverage equal to fifty percent or more of the Coverage A limit. The amount of insurance for Coverage C can be increased. An amount equal to ten percent of the Coverage C limit is available for loss to property usually located at a residence other than the listed residence.

Coverage D — Provides for additional living expenses of the insured in the event of loss or for the loss of fair rental value if a direct loss occurs to a part of the dwelling rented to others. It is an additional amount equal to thirty percent of the amount of insurance selected for Coverage A. In many policies the coverage is available only for a limited period of time such as one year following the loss.

Coverage E — Provides personal liability protection against the financial consequences of acts for which an insured may be held legally liable. The combined single limit of $100,000 covering bodily injury and property damage liability can be increased for an additional premium.

Coverage F — Medical payments insurance for noninsured individuals injured by the insured, or while on the insured premises, or by someone or something under the control of the insured. There is no requirement that the insured be legally liable for the coverage to apply to an injured party. Reasonable medical expenses will be paid for up to three years for medical, surgical, x-ray, dental, ambulance, hospital, professional nursing, prosthetic devices and funeral services. Coverage is $1,000 for each person injured but can be increased for an additional premium.

HOMEOWNERS POLICY FORMS.

There are six policy forms from which the applicant/insured may select. The forms are designated as to the type of property to be insured and the causes of loss (perils) which are included. Personal liability and medical payments are included on all six policy forms.

HO-2 - Broad Form — Provides Broad Causes of Loss for an Owner/Occupant of a dwelling including the dwelling, other structures and personal property.

HO-3 - Special Form — The form affords Special Causes of Loss on the dwelling and Broad Form Perils on personal property for an Owner/Occupant of a dwelling.

HO-4 - Contents Broad Form — This policy form is for those who rent an apartment, condominium or single family dwelling. Coverages A and B do not apply but the remaining coverages are the same as the HO-3.

HO-5 - Comprehensive Form — Provides Special Causes of Loss on the dwelling, other structures and personal property for an owner/occupant.

HO-6 - Unit Owner's Form — This policy form meets the insurance requirements of condominium and cooperative apartment owners. Coverage A applies to alterations, appliances and improvements that are part of the building and contained within the resident's premises. There is no Coverage B but the rest of the HO-3 coverages are included.

HO-8 - Modified Coverage Form — This form is used when the owner-occupant of dwellings does not meet the standards required for other forms.

ENDORSEMENT FOR THE HOMEOWNERS PROGRAM.

There are a number of endorsements available for the Homeowners policies which can increase, decrease or modify coverage for the Homeowners Program which is a self-contained policy.

An example is the Personal Property Replacement Cost Loss Settlement endorsement which provides replacement cost for personal property. The dwelling and other structures are already covered for replacement cost under the policy.

Other endorsements include the Inflation Guard Endorsement, Structures Rented to Others endorsement, Permitted Incidental Occupancies — Residence Premises endorsement and the Home Day Care Coverage endorsement.

ADDITIONAL COVERAGE UNDER THE HOMEOWNERS PROGRAM.

Coverage is extended to a variety of loss exposures under the Homeowners program. The amount of insurance for these exposures may be "in addition to" or "included in" the policy limits. Some of these coverages are found in the A, B, C or D coverages while others reinstate items that were excluded under the coverages. However, an insured's policy should be reviewed to determine the existence of such coverages and any limits they may have.

These additional coverages are: Debris Removal, Reasonable Repairs, Fire Department Service Charge, Property Removed, Credit Card, Electronic Fund Transfer Card or Access Device, Forgery and Counterfeit Money, Loss Assessment, Collapse, Glass or Safety Glazing Material, Landlord's Furnishings, Ordinance or Law, Grave Markers, and Trees, Shrubs and Other Plants.

CONDITIONS AFFECTING THE HOMEOWNERS POLICIES.

General policy conditions. — These apply to both Section I and II and include: Policy period, concealment or fraud, liberalization clause, waiver or change, cancellation, nonrenewal, subrogation and death provision.

Loss settlement conditions. — Included are: insurable interest and limit of liability, duties after a loss, loss settlement, loss to pair or set, glass replacement, appraisal, other insurance, suit against the insurance company, our option, loss payment, abandonment of property, mortgage clause, no benefit to bailee, nuclear hazard clause, recovered property and volcanic eruption period.

EXCLUSIONS AFFECTING THE HOMEOWNERS POLICIES.

The Homeowners policy like other property and liability insurance policies has Exclusions and Exceptions that can ultimately affect a loss settlement. A number of these exclusions are identified here. However, the actual existence and wording of these items should be reviewed in the insured's policy.

General exclusions are: Ordinance or law, Earth movement, Water damage, Power failure, Neglect, War, Nuclear hazard and Intentional loss. Other exclusions are Collapse, Freezing of a plumbing, heating, air conditioning, sprinkler system or household appliance, Freezing, thawing, pressure, or weight of water or ice, Theft of construction materials, Vandalism and malicious mischief to vacant dwellings, Mold, fungus, or wet rot, Natural deterioration, Smoke from agricultural smudging or industrial operations, Pollutants, Settling of the dwelling, and Animals.

An ensuing loss caused by an excluded event, such as a flood, may be covered unless the ensuing loss is also excluded. This is a situation that is determined following a loss to the property.

Exclusions designed to respond to the problem of "Concurrent causation" are weather conditions, acts or omissions of any person, group, organization or governmental body and activities performed in a faulty manner to cause loss.

DWELLING PROGRAM.

Some residences are not eligible for the Homeowners Program because of their value, occupancy or an underwriting reason. Also it may be that

---

the owner does not want the full range of coverages of the Homeowners Program nor want to pay the higher premiums. Such properties can be insured under the Dwelling Program (DP).

There are three forms—DP-1, DP-2 and DP-3 which are similar to the insuring agreements and definitions of Section I of the Homeowners forms. There is no reference to liability or medical payments coverage as they are not included in the Dwelling Program. The Dwelling forms are mono-line policies.

The coverage parts are: Coverage A — Dwelling, Coverage B — Other Structures, Coverage C — Personal Property, Coverage D — Fair Rental Value and Coverage E — Additional Living Expense.

The insured selects a dollar amount for Coverage A and a dollar amount for Coverage B. For Coverage D and E there is automatic coverage equal to 20 percent of the dollar amount for Coverage A for each of them.

The perils insured against generally correspond with those in the Homeowners forms except that theft coverage is not included. The Personal Liability supplement can be used to provide personal liability (Coverage L) and Medical Payments to Others (Coverage M). Residential Theft coverage can be added by endorsement providing either Broad theft coverage (owner occupied) or Limited theft coverage (not owner occupied). Policy exclusions and conditions are also similar to the Homeowners program.

The Dwelling Form can be used to provide coverage for the owner of a dwelling or condominium who is renting the property to another party. The tenant could then purchase a HO-4 Tenants Form to cover its loss exposure. Also dwelling policies can also be used for 1) dwellings under construction, 2) mobile homes at a permanent location, 3) houseboats, in some states and 4) some incidental business occupancies when used by the owner/insured or by a tenant.

MOBILE HOME INSURANCE.

Mobile homes, also called Manufacture Housing, are used in areas where smaller and less expensive housing is in demand such as rural, retirement and vacation areas. These units are considered as personal property because of their mobile nature.

Some insurance companies have their own form while others use the Mobile Home Form (MH 04 01) attached to the HO-3 this is an owner/occupied form. If the unit were rented then the owner would need a dwelling coverage form and the tenant would need a renter's policy.

The form includes Coverage A — Dwelling, Coverage B — Other Structures, Coverage C — Personal Property and Coverage D — Loss of use. Coverage B limit is an amount equal to 10 percent the amount of Coverage A while Coverage C is 40 percent and Coverage D is 20 percent. Perils insured against are the same as the HO-3 as are the exclusions.

Under "Additional Coverages" there is a provision for up to $500 to cover reasonable expenses incurred to remove and return the mobile home if threatened by a covered peril. No deductible applies.

There are a number of endorsements available such as Actual Cash Value, Transportation/Permission to Move, Mobile Home Lienholders' Single Interest, Property Removed Increase Limit and Ordinance or Law Coverage.

THE NATIONAL FLOOD INSURANCE PROGRAM.

The National Flood Insurance Program (NFIP) provides insurance coverage for eligible properties in designated communities. The program is administered by the Federal Insurance Administration of the Federal Emergency Management Agency (FEMA) and is available in all states, Puerto Rico, Guam and the U.S. Virgin Islands.

Private insurance companies also sell this flood insurance under their own names, collect the premiums, retain a specified percentage for commissions and expenses and service the policy. However, the federal government is responsible for loss costs under these policies. The amount of coverage available under the NFIP is $500,000.

Private flood insurance also is available through insurance companies on properties that they are willing to insure. The coverage is written by endorsement to commercial policies and with a high deductible. In some cases the private insurance policies are written as excess over the NFIP program coverage.

FAIR PLAN, BEACHFRONT & WINDSTORM PLANS.

Government efforts to assist property owners who are unable to obtain insurance in the private market have resulted in the development of the Fair Access to Insurance Requirements (FAIR) plans and Beachfront and Windstorm plans.

The FAIR Plans. — To request coverage under the FAIR plan the applicant must not be eligible for insurance in the voluntary market and the property must first be inspected. Coverage can then be accepted, accepted with required repairs or denied by the plan. The coverage provided may be limited to fire and some specified perils or to a limited homeowners policy. The plans are issued by the states and can vary in coverage as do the procedures involved.

Beachfront and Windstorm Plans. — These plans are similar in design as the FAIR plan and make insurance available to those properties in designated areas for windstorm and hail losses. Properties must be ineligible for coverage in the voluntary market and meet other requirements of the plan. In some areas there are state run property insurance companies that provide coverage for beachfront windstorms. The general area involved in these programs is the east coast and the Gulf coast.

COMMERCIAL PROPERTY COVERAGE.

Commercial property insurance provides coverage for buildings and their contents that suffer direct loss from a covered peril as well as coverage for the loss of income due to the interruption of business and necessary extra expenses.

The Commercial Package Policy (CPP) consisting of a Common Policy Conditions Form and a Common Declarations Form to which Coverage Parts such as the Commercial Property coverage part are attached.

Each Coverage Part consists of a Declaration form, Coverage form, General Provisions form and any necessary endorsements. A Coverage Part can be used in the CPP or as a monoline policy.

BUILDING AND PERSONAL PROPERTY COVERAGE FORM (BPP).

The Building and Personal Property Coverage Form (BPP) provides property insurance for commercial buildings and their contents. It is part of the Commercial Package Policy (CPP) program and may also be written as a monoline policy.

The BPP covers buildings and business personal property (of the insured) as well as personal property of others, but only when a limit of insurance is shown for the coverage on the declarations form.

Buildings are described by location, construction, and occupancy. The term "building" is defined in the policy to include the structure, completed additions, permanently installed items (fixtures, machinery, equipment), outdoor fixtures and personal property of the insured used to maintain or service the building.

If not covered by other insurance policies, additions, alterations or repairs to the building as well as the necessary materials, equipment and supplies are also included.

Business Personal property of the insured. — There are two areas involved with this coverage. The first is property owned by the insured. The second is property owned by others which has an incidental exposure associated with the main exposure insured.

Personal property of others. — This is a separate section of coverage that can provide an additional limit of insurance when needed for such property. It will pay the owner of the property for loss or damage regardless of the insured's liability.

Limitations and Exclusions. — The coverage form restricts coverage under the policy for certain types of property including the following:

Other real property. — Included here are land, water, bridges, roadways, retaining walls, docks, cost of excavations, pilings, foundations below grade, and underground pipes. Any of these excluded items can be covered for an additional charge except land and water.

Plants and outdoor property. — This exclusion includes growing crops, lawns, harvested crops, trees, shrubs, plants, fences, antennas and signs except signs attached to buildings. Some exposures have limited coverage provided in the coverage extensions. All of these can be insured by endorsement or by other insurance forms.

Other personal property. — Although excluded these areas can generally be insured by endorsement or on another form. The first group includes: Accounts, Bills, Currency, Deeds, Evidence of debts, Money and Securities. They can usually be covered under inland marine forms. (Editor's note: One can remember these as the "A, B, C, D, E, and M/S" exclusions). Also excluded are food stamps and lottery tickets. Theft coverage for lottery tickets is limited to $250 under the Causes of Loss—Special Form).

The second group includes aircraft, watercraft, vehicles, animals, valuable papers and records, property otherwise covered and contraband. Vehicles manufactured and held for sale (except autos) can be covered as well as animals held for sale (except farm animals). Personal property while airborne or waterborne is excluded but can be insured under transit policies.

Locations and Limitations. — The policy restricts coverage to property at the described locations with some limited exceptions.

Business Personal Property and Personal Property of Others. — Both are covered in the open or in a vehicle within 100 feet of the insured premises. The term "within 100 feet of the insured premises" has been determined to mean within 100 feet of the nearest boundary of the land considered to be part of the insured premises not just within 100 feet of the building.

However, there are two extensions of coverage for property located away from the described premises.

Property Off-Premises. — There is limited coverage at other locations within the policy territory (United States, its territories and possessions, Puerto Rico and Canada).

Newly Acquired or Constructed Property. — Coverage is also provided for additional properties obtained after the policy's effective date with some limitations.

Supplemental Coverages. — There are two groups of supplemental coverages under the BPP coverage form. These are Additional coverages and Coverage extensions.

Additional coverages. — Included are Debris removal, Pollution cleanup and removal, Preservation of property and Fire department service charge.

Coverage extensions. — These include Newly acquired or constructed property, Personal effects and property of others, Valuable papers and records (cost of research), Property off premises and Outdoor property.

The coverage extensions are in addition to the applicable policy limit and are subject to internal limits of liability. Some may be increased by endorsement or covered under inland marine forms.

Limitations on Insurance Coverage. — The BPP includes provisions that address the limits of insurance, the deductible and coinsurance when dealing with a covered loss.

Limits of insurance and deductible. — The limits apply to each occurrence with no annual aggregate limit (except for the pollution cleanup and removal coverage). The limits reinstate after each loss. The limit of insurance applies after the deductible. That is if the insured had loss of $51,000 with a $1,000 deductible and $50,000 limits the policy limit of $50,000 would be paid.

Coinsurance. — The coinsurance clause is simply a device to require insureds to purchase insurance to value. Otherwise many would buy only the amount they felt they might lose and the insurance company would not receive the premium base needed. In return for a reduced premium rate the insured agrees to carry insurance at least equal to a specific percentage of the actual cash value of the property (at the time of loss) or suffer a penalty. Coinsurance percentages of 80, 90 and 100 are commonly used.

The formula used to determine if the insurance required is adequate is as follows: Amount Carried/Amount Required x Coinsurance Percent x Amount of Loss - Deductible = Amount of Loss Payment

For example a building is insured for $80,000 with an 80 percent coinsurance clause. At the time of loss the amount of insurance required is determine to be $100,000. The deductible is $1,000. The loss is $40,000. The loss payment is calculated: $80,000/$100,000 x $40,000 = $32,000 - $1,000 = $31,000.

It is important to remember to use the Actual Cash Value of the property at the time of loss in determining the amount of insurance required. Also, the amount of loss paid will never exceed policy limits.

Methods of Valuation. — In the BPP the methods of valuation used differ because of the several types of property. The methods used are:

Actual Cash Value (ACV). — Under this approach the replacement cost (RC) of the property (at the time of loss) is determined and depreciation (D) is taken. The result is the actual cash value of the property at the time of loss. (RC - D = ACV).

Depreciation. — It is often difficult for an insurance company to determine depreciation and can be equally confusing to the insured. An example is a roof damaged by a windstorm. If the roof had a useful life of 20 years and was damaged during the 10th year after it was installed the cost to replace the roof would be depreciated fifty percent. (Example - 10/20 = .50)

Small losses. — Under the building coverage losses are paid on a repair or replacement cost with no deductible if under $2,500. Some items excluded from this method include awnings, floor covering, appliances and outdoor equipment.

Tenants Improvements and Betterments. — The improvements and betterments made by an insured tenant are covered at actual cash value if repaired or replaced. If they are not repaired then the insured tenant can only recover the remaining use value which is a percentage of the original cost.

Additional Loss Provisions. — The BPP includes several additional loss provisions that are designed to address various activities.

Duties of the insured in the event a loss include: Notice of loss — Promptly provide information as soon as reasonably possible, Police report — If a law has been broken, Preservation of property — To protect it from further loss costs are paid under limit, Inventory and inspection — Complete inventory and permit inspection with any costs involved not paid under coverage, Proof of loss — Signed and sworn proof within 60 days after receiving forms and Examination under oath — May be taken by insurance company and signed by insured.

Appraisal. — When either party disputes the value of the claim an appraisal can be requested. Each party selects an appraiser and those two select an umpire. The appraisers each value the loss and if they do not agree, submit their findings to the umpire. A decision by any two of the three is binding on the insurance company and the insured. If there is still disagreement, the matter can be moved to the courts.

Insurance company's options for loss payment. — In addition to paying for repairs or replacement or paying the value of the property, the insurance company has two other options. It may take all or any part of the property and pay an agreed or appraised price. Also the insurance company can have the repairs made or replace it with property of like kind and quality.

Recovered property. — If either party recovers any of the property following settlement it must notify the other promptly. The insured can demand return of the property but must also return any loss payment. The insurance company pays for any repair and recovery expense.

Vacancy. — A building is "vacant" when it does not contain enough business personal property to conduct customary operations otherwise it is simply "unoccupied." When it is vacant after sixty consecutive days there is no coverage for vandalism, sprinkler leakage, building glass breakage, water damage, theft or attempted theft. Loss by any other peril is reduced by 15 percent after sixty days of vacancy.

BUSINESS INCOME INSURANCE (BIC).

A property loss at many commercial properties will result in a reduction in income generated by the property due to the interruption of business following the loss. To cover the chance that such a loss would take place property owners will seek to cover the risk through Business Income Insurance (BIC).

A loss caused by the interruption of business would be covered if it is caused by property damage from an insured peril to buildings and business personal property at locations or activities described in the policy which results in a loss of business income and/or extra expense.

Such losses are considered as a reduction in Net Income which is the difference between Revenues and Expenses. When net income is positive it is deemed to be Profit. If net income is negative the result is a Net Loss.

Business Income Insurance provides coverage for the reduction in net income which is the result of a loss to an insured's building and personal property. The loss is based on the amount of lost income which is determined by subtracting the amount of income received during the period of interruption from the "Expected Income" during that period.

During a period of interruption three things can occur 1) there will be continuing expenses, 2) there will be non-continuing expenses and 3) there may be extra expenses. It can be difficult to determine which business expenses may continue and which expenses may not continue. Extra expenses are those which help to lessen the effects of the business interruption.

The Business Income form provides that the insured can select from 1) Business Income including Rental Value, 2) Business Income other than Rental Value or 3) Rental Value only depending on the needs of the business.

Additional coverages under the BIC include loss caused by action of a Civil Authority, loss caused by delay of starting operations in new buildings or alterations to existing buildings, extended business income beyond the period of restoration and the interruption of computer operations caused by a covered loss. There is a coverage extension for newly acquired buildings.

Settlement of a business income loss involves determining the actual loss of business income sustained caused by the suspension of operations during a period of restoration caused by the direct physical loss or damage to the insured property.

BUSINESSOWNERS POLICY.

The Businessowners Policy (BOP) is a multi-peril package policy for small and medium size commercial properties. It is similar in scope to the personal lines Homeowners Program.

The types of property covered include buildings, business personal property, personal property of others, business income and extra expense. Also included in the policy coverages are premises and operations liability, products and completed operations liability, contractual liability and personal and advertising injury liability. Other coverages are employee dishonest, theft of money and securities, and forgery and alteration. Finally the equipment breakdown exposure is included.

While commercial owned auto coverage is not included in the BOP it is possible to add hired and nonowned auto coverage. Other coverages desired by the insured can be endorsed on the policy.

There are restrictions on what types of property are eligible for the BOP. These are based on occupancy, total floor area, height of structure, annual gross sales, as well as the business type and operations.

The rating procedure is based on the amount of building and personal property coverage while the liability rating involves the class of business insured.

FARM INSURANCE POLICY.

The Farm Insurance policy is designed to provide coverage for family farm operations as well as commercial farm exposures. The policy is modular and resembles the Homeowners policy. It can be written as a monoline policy or as a package policy.

The Farm Property–Farm Dwellings, Appurtenant Structure and Household Personal Property Coverage Form has the following coverages: Coverage A — Dwelling, Coverage B — Structures Appurtenant to Dwellings, Coverage C — Household Personal Property and Coverage D — Loss of Use.

The Farm Property-Farm Personal Property Coverage Form includes both Coverage E — Scheduled Farm Personal Property and Coverage F — Unscheduled Farm Personal Property coverages. An insured may select either or both depending on need.

The Farm Property-Barns, Outbuildings and Other Farm Structures Form includes Coverage G which is used to cover all structures other than dwellings.

The causes of loss forms for this policy are the Basic, Broad and Special forms. Depending on which form is used livestock and other farm animals have various levels of coverage.

Because of the limitations of standard farm policies there are also Specialty Farm Coverages such as crop-hail insurance, federal crop insurance and animal mortality insurance available for farm owners, ranchers and non-farm owners of valuable animals.

CHAPTER THREE

BASIC PRINCIPLES & CONCEPTS OF LIABILITY INSURANCE

INTRODUCTION.

The purpose of Liability Insurance is to protect an insured from economic loss in the event the insured is negligent and held legally liable for causing injury to other parties or damage to the property of others. There are many forms of liability insurance that are designed to respond to different types of needs. Some policies provide insurance coverage for individuals while others cover commercial or professional activities.

PRINCIPLES OF TORT LAW.

Liability insurance deals with Tort Law and the concept of Negligence. A "tort" is a wrongful act or omission that invades the legally protected right of another party. The at-fault party is called a tortfeasor.

The elements of a tort are: 1) a legally protected right, 2) the wrongful invasion of that right and 3) damages as a proximate or direct result of that invasion.

There are two basic types of torts. First are those torts, which involve injury to the person and the other are those torts that cause injury to property. The following represent torts that cause injury to the person:

Assault. — Here the act requires only that one party makes a threat to injure another party.

Battery. — This tort is often used in conjunction with Assault and means the actual physical striking of another.

Invasion of Privacy. — This occurs when an individual's privacy is either obstructed or invaded by another party.

Defamation of Character. — It can occur either through the written word (libel) or the spoken word (slander).

False Arrest. — This usually takes place when an individual is wrongly accused of a crime. For example a person is arrested for shoplifting but is found innocent. The injured party could file a false arrest action against the retailer.

Of the five torts that involve injury to the person Assault and Batter cannot be insured and are excluded from liability policies. The other three can be insured under Personal Injury Liability coverage.

The following represent torts that cause injury to property:

Trespass. — A tort which injures property. However the act of trespassing must be malicious. An unintentional trespass of another's property is not considered a serious offense.

Conversion. — Is taking of property of another as one's own while knowing it does not belong to you. An individual takes a friend's wall clock home to repair it and then rather than returning it places the clock on his own wall. The "repairman" has converted the clock to his own use.

CONCEPT OF NEGLIGENCE.

When an individual fails to act as a reasonable and prudent person would have acted under similar circumstances, that individual may be held to have been negligent. The decision as to whether an at-fault party was negligent is generally determined by a court of law. The penalty for negligence is money damages.

An at-fault party can be held liable for negligence only if the injured party can prove all the following elements of negligence: 1) The at-fault party owed a legal duty to the plaintiff to use due care, 2) The at-fault party breached the legal duty owed to the injured party, 3) The injured party suffered actual damage and 4) There was a proximate or close causal connection between the at-fault party's negligent act and the resulting damage to the injured party.

Proximate Cause. — A continuous unbroken chain of events without which the end results would not have happened. It begins with the covered peril and ends with an injured party or damaged property. Such cause is not necessarily the nearest in time or in the sequence of events just as long as it is the superior or controlling factor, the one which sets the intervening conditions in motion.

Degrees of negligence. — It is the extent of the negligent act which can affect the penalty assessed against the at-fault party. It includes the following:

Simple Negligence. — The at-fault part was negligent but there was no apparent intent to cause injury or damage to the other party.

Willful and Wanton Negligence. — The at-fault party failed to heed a warning and caused an injury or damage.

Contributory Negligence. — Two individuals are held to have both been negligent in the act that caused injury or damage. Neither can collect damage from the other.

Comparative Negligence. — Two individuals are involved in an act that caused injury or damage. The situation is reviewed to determine the percent of damage caused by the actions of each party. For example, if the injured party was 30 percent at fault the other party would be responsible for only 70 percent of the damages.

Absolute Negligence. — Under this concept of negligence, one party is held to be negligent regardless of the acts of the injured party. An example is an employer who is held to be absolutely negligent under Workers Compensation laws if an employee is injured by an act "arising out of and in the course of employment."

A party claiming injury by a negligent act must establish that actual damages of a type recognized by law and measured as money damages did occur. These factors include:

Compensatory damages. — The total of monetary loss experienced by the injured party are the compensatory damages and can include special damages and general damages. Special damages include such items as medical expense, cost to repair or replace damaged property and loss of earnings. General damages represent an amount to compensate for intangible loss claimed by the injured party such as pain and suffering, mental anguish and bereavement.

Punitive damages. — These may be imposed upon the at-fault party to punish, teach a lesson or to deter others from the same kind of conduct. Punitive damages are not covered by insurance in many jurisdictions.

FRAMEWORK OF A LIABILITY POLICY.

There are many features of a liability policy that are common to all types of liability policies. It is important to understand this framework.

First, the liability policy sets forth that this insurance provides coverage against all claims of Bodily Injury, Sickness or Disease or Damage to Property including Loss of Use thereof which are the result of negligent acts of the insured. Most liability policies also provide legal defense against any alleged claim regardless of whether or not such claim is valid, false or fraudulent.

The policy describes both Bodily Injury and Property Damage liability insurance that are two of the coverages included in the policy. Another coverage which is included in most liability policies is Medical Payments.

It is by the "Insuring Agreement" that the difference between various types of liability policies is established. The policy itself indicates how the legal liability must be caused; i.e., by the operation, maintenance or use of an automobile or by some other activity such as the use of a product or by a professional activity.

A Limit of Liability is established for each type of coverage in the contract based upon the premium charged. For example, if the Bodily Injury limits are stated as $100,000 per person and $300,000 per occurrence, the premium would be higher than if the limits were $25,000 per person and $50,000 per occurrence. There would be separate limits stated for the Property Damage coverage.

This type of limit is called a Split Limit which means that no one person could recover more than the per person limit. Also no more than the per occurrence limit would be paid for all claims resulting to all persons injured in the same occurrence.

Another form of liability limit is the Combined Single Limit where there is neither a per person or a per occurrence limit. It only has a single dollar amount from with either bodily injury or property damage claims or both can be paid.

Under a liability policy, there is coverage for each separate occurrence. For example it would cover a loss today and another tomorrow at the full policy limits. However, liability policies have an aggregate limit which is the total amount that the insurance company will pay in losses during a single policy year for that type of insurance.

For example, a policy might pay out $45,000 for a Bodily Injury claim in January and in July have another Bodily Injury claim for $65,000 but if the policy aggregate limit for Bodily Injury was only $100,000 the insured would be responsible for $15,000. This would be because the $65,000 was in excess of the $50,000 per person limit and also it was in excess of the $100,000 aggregate limit ($45,000 + $65,000).

The policy coverage for any loss under a liability policy is subject to the provisions, conditions and exclusions found in the policy.

LIABILTY INSURANCE POLICIES.

Liability Insurance Policies provide insurance for individuals and commercial organizations by utilizing insurance coverage for specific types of losses. Personal liability loss exposures are covered within the Homeowners policy and the Personal Auto policy. The Commercial liability policies provide insurance for business and professional loss exposures such as the Commercial General Liability (CGL) policy and Professional Liability policies. The liability insurance policy that is most common is the Personal Auto Policy (PAP) which will be discussed next.

PERSONAL AUTO INSURANCE.

The Personal Auto Policy (PAP) provides coverage for loss exposures that arise out of the ownership, maintenance or use of an automobile. Eligible types of vehicles include private passenger autos, minivans and sport utility vehicles owned by the insured.

Pickup trucks and vans can be insured under the PAP if the vehicle has a gross weight of less than 10,000 pounds and is not used for the delivery or transportation of goods and materials. There is coverage for pickup trucks if the use is incidental to the insured's business of installing, maintaining or repairing furnishings or equipment or when used for farming or ranching.

The Personal Auto Policy can also be endorsed to cover motorcycles, golf carts, snowmobiles and similar vehicles. Newly acquired vehicles, while automatically covered for liability exposures, must be reported within 14 days. A replacement vehicle is insured for the remainder of the policy period with the same coverages as the replaced vehicle.

In addition to owned vehicles an insured may be using a nonowned vehicle, such as a rented car or may be using a temporary substitute auto because the insured's vehicle is out of service. The PAP provides limited coverage on such vehicles.

Parties insured under the PAP. – 1) The named insured and any family member, 2) Any person using the named insured's covered auto with permission, 3) Any person or organization but only for legal liability arising out of the insured's use of a covered auto on behalf of that person or organization and 4) A family member as identified in the policy declarations.

Structure of the PAP. — The policy is made up of a Declarations page, Agreement and Definitions page and the following parts: Part A — Liability Coverage, Part B — Medical Payments Coverage, Part C — Uninsured Motorists Coverage, Part D — Coverage for Damage to Your Auto, Part E — Duties After an Accident of Loss and Part F — General Provisions.

Part A — Liability coverage. — The insurance company agrees to pay for bodily injury or property damage for which the insured becomes legally responsible due to an automobile accident. It can be issued with a single limit or split limits. The policy also provides legal defense costs in addition to the policy limit and supplementary payments such as premiums on bail and attachment bonds and $200 per day for loss of earnings if required to attend hearings or trials.

Liability coverage exclusions for the PAP include: intentional injury committed by using the vehicle, property owned or transported in the insured vehicle such as personal property, personal property is also excluded but this exclusion does not apply to damage to a rented residence or private garage, bodily injury to an employee of a covered person, using the vehicle as a public or livery conveyance but this exclusion does not apply to use of the vehicle in a car pool and property rented, used or in the care of the insured.

Part B — Medical Payments coverage. — This section provides for all reasonable and necessary medical, surgical, dental and funeral expenses faced by an insured resulting from bodily injury caused by accident and incurred within three years of the date of accident. The coverage is available for each insured person who is injured in, getting into, on, out or off of an insured vehicle and applies without regard to fault.

An insured person for medical payments coverage includes the named insured and family members and any other person while occupying a covered automobile. The named insured and family member are also covered if injured as a pedestrian and struck by a motor vehicle designed for use mainly on public roads.

Part C — Uninsured Motorists and Underinsured Motorists Liability insurance (UM/UIM). — These coverages are designed to meet the financial problems incurred due to bodily injury suffered by the insured which was caused by the negligent act of an uninsured or underinsured motorist.

Persons insured under UM/UIM include the named insured and family members, any other person occupying a covered auto and any person legally entitled to recover damages (such as the widow of an insured killed in an auto accident by an at-fault UM/UIM driver).

An uninsured motorist (UM) includes a negligent uninsured motorist, a hit-and-run driver or at-fault driver whose auto insurance company becomes insolvent.

The underinsured motorist (UIM) is an at-fault driver who has insurance but with liability limits lower than those of the insured. The injured insured can collect the difference between the two limits when the underinsured motorist is held liable.

When the insurance company and the insured cannot agree as to the damages or the amount of damage under a UM/UIM loss the matter can be settled by submitting the matter to arbitration.

Part D — Damage to Your Auto. — This coverage includes the physical damage insurance Collision Loss and Other Than Collision. The former covers damage caused by collision or upset. The latter is often called "Comprehensive" and includes coverage for fire, theft, windstorm, flood, riot, vandalism, contact with a bird or animal and glass breakage losses.

When an insured is using a nonowned vehicle, which is not furnished or available for the insured's regular use, the physical damage coverages apply to the nonowned vehicle but only on an excess basis. The physical damage coverages that apply to an insured's owned auto will apply to a temporary substitute vehicle used by the insured.

Part E — Duties After an Accident or Loss. — These provisions set forth the general duties expected of the insured when loss occurs as well as some specific duties for Uninsured Motorists claims and Physical Damage losses.

Part F — General Provisions. — Matters such as changes in the policy, legal actions against the company, policy period and territory, termination and the insurance company's right to recover payment from an at-fault driver are covered in this section.

Residual Auto Insurance Market. — In addition to the standard automobile insurance market there is the residual market available for drivers that cannot otherwise obtain auto insurance. These markets are the Automobile Insurance Plan (Assigned Risk Plan) and Specialty Insurance Companies. Premiums are generally higher than the standard market and may be limited or restricted by state law. An insured person under the Automobile Insurance Plan is placed with an insurance company that will handle the policy and any claims. After a period of three years the insured may be able to reenter the private insurance market for coverage.

COMMERCIAL GENERAL LIABILITY.

The Commercial General Liability (CGL) policy is the basic liability insurance available to businesses and other organizations. The policy provides financial protection in the event the insured is held legally liable for injury to others or damage to the property of another. The CGL can be issued as part of a Commercial Package Policy (CPP) or as a monoline contract.

The general categories of liability loss exposures in the CGL form are Coverage A — Bodily Injury and Property Damage Liability and Coverage B — Personal and Advertising Injury Liability. In addition the policy includes Coverage C — Medical Payments and several Supplementary Payments.

Coverage A — Bodily Injury and Property Damage. — Under this section the policy will pay for Bodily Injury or Property Damage to a third-party for which the insured is legally liable and was caused by an "Occurrence" during the policy period. An Occurrence is defined as "an accident, including continuous or repeated exposure to substantially the same general harmful conditions."

The types of losses under Coverage A include those which occur on the insured's premises or out of the insured's operations. They may also be caused by a product or by completed operations of the insured. There is also coverage for liability assumed by contract. Fire legal liability coverage is included in the policy.

The loss must result from bodily injury or property damage to which the coverage applies, caused by an occurrence, in the coverage territory, during the policy period. In addition the insurance company has a duty to defend the insured with the legal costs being in addition to the policy limits. The coverage territory is the United States, its territories and possessions, Puerto Rico and Canada. Coverage for products liability is worldwide.

Coverage B — Personal and Advertising Injury. — This insurance provides coverage for injury caused by the loss of reputation, humiliation, economic loss, and consequential bodily injury caused by an offense such as false arrest, wrongful eviction, libel, slander and infringing on another's copyright in the insured's advertising. While the coverage is included in the policy the insured has the option of purchasing it or not.

Coverage C — Medical Payments — Coverage is available for the medical expense of others under certain circumstances. As it does not require the insured to be liable it is not technically liability insurance. The injury must have been caused by bodily injury due to an accident on the insureds premises or as the result of the insured's operations anywhere in the policy territory.

Policy exclusions. — Under Coverage A exclusions include: Expected or intended injury, Contractual liability (with exceptions), Liquor liability, Workers compensation and employers liability, Pollution, Aircraft, Auto or Watercraft, Mobile equipments (with exceptions), War, Damage to property, Insured's products and work, Damage to your product, Damage to your work, Damage to impaired property or property not physically injured, Personal and advertising injury, Electronic data, Distribution of material in violation of statutes and Recall of products, work or impaired property.

Coverage B exclusions that are unique to the coverage are: Knowing violation of rights of another, Material published with knowledge of falsity, Material published prior to policy period, Criminal acts, Contractual liability, Breach of contract, Quality or performance of goods, Failure to conform to statements, Wrong description of prices, Insured in media and internet type businesses, Electronic chatrooms or bulletin boards, Unauthorized use of another's name or product, Pollution, Pollution-related, War, Distribution of material in violation of statutes and Infringement of copyright, patent, trademark or trade secret.

Who is an Insured? — The named insured can be an individual, partnership, joint venture, corporation, limited liability company or a trust. The named insured, if an individual, includes a spouse for business ventures. If a partnership or joint venture then the named partner and all other partners and their spouses are insureds for business activities. For a corporation all executives, officers, directors and stockholders are insureds but only while conducting business for the corporation.

Others who are insureds with limitations under the CGL include named insured's employees and volunteer workers, other persons and organizations, real estate managers, legal representatives and newly acquired organizations.

Coverage Triggers. — There are two forms of CGL based on the coverage trigger. The first and most common trigger is the Occurrence Form which covers losses that occur during the policy period regardless of when reported. The second is the Claims-Made Form which requires that the claim both occur and be reported during the policy period. The Occurrence Form is the most common.

BUSINESS AUTO INSURANCE.

Businesses can face liability from the use of owned, hired, and borrowed autos or an auto owned by an employee and used in the business. Also a business may assume the auto liability of another firm through a contract. The Business Auto Coverage form can include optional physical damage insurance and by endorsement uninsured and underinsured liability as well as medical payments can be added.

The Business Auto Coverage Form (BACF) can be issued as part of a Commercial Package Policy (CPP) or as a monoline policy.

The parts of the BACF are: Section I — Covered Autos, Section II — Liability Coverage, Section III — Physical Damage Coverage, Section IV — Business Auto Conditions and Section V — Definitions.

The policy can be used to insure the automobile liability exposure of most commercial businesses with two exceptions. These are "auto businesses" and "motor carriers for hire" for which coverage is available in the Garage Coverage Form and the Motor Carrier Coverage Form.

Section I of the policy has descriptive symbols which represent the motor vehicle to be insured by type, use or other requirements. A policy may have vehicles listed under more than one symbol as the make up of a fleet can vary.

The ten symbols are: Symbol 1 - Any Auto, Symbol 2 - Owned Autos Only, Symbol 3 - Owned Private Passenger Autos Only, Symbol 4 - Owned Autos Other Than Private Passenger Autos Only, Symbol 5 - Owned Autos Subject to No-Fault, Symbol 6 - Owned Autos Subject to a Compulsory Uninsured Motorist Law, Symbol 7 - Specifically Described Autos, Symbol 8 - Hired Autos Only, Symbol 9 - Nonowned Autos Only and Symbol 19 - Mobil Equipment Subject to Compulsory or Financial Responsibility or Other Motor Vehicle Insurance Law Only.

In addition the policy has a Schedule of Coverages which allows the insured to select coverages for each of the Symbols that apply. Included are liability, auto medical payments, physical damage and uninsured and underinsured motorists coverages and others.

The named insured is the insured for any covered vehicle. Anyone with permission is an insured for a covered owned auto or one that is hired or borrowed by the named insured.

Some exclusions are: Expected or Intended injury, Contractual Liability (with exceptions), Worker Compensation and Related Exclusions, Exclusions Related to Loading and Unloading, Operations and Completed Operations Exclusions and Pollution, War, Racing and Care, Custody and Control exclusions.

Conditions applicable to the BACF include: Loss Conditions — Appraisal for Physical Damage Losses, Legal Action Against the Insurer, Loss Payment-Physical Damage Coverages, Transfer of Rights Against Others and Duties in the Event of an Accident, Claim, Suit or Loss.

General Conditions — Bankruptcy, Concealment, Misrepresentation, or Fraud, Liberalization, No Benefit to Bailee-Physical Damage Insurance Only, Other Insurance, Premium Audit, Policy Period, Coverage Territory and Two or More Coverage Forms or Policies Issued by the Insurer.

GARAGE AND MOTOR CARRIER INSURANCE.

For those businesses with unique auto insurance needs, the following forms have been developed and are used rather than the Business Auto Policy.

GARAGE COVERAGE FORM.

This form is used to insure auto and trailer dealers who deal in sales and service. While considered commercial auto coverage the form combines commercial general liability, business auto liability and physical damage coverages in a single policy. The three sections of the policy are:

Liability Coverage. — There are two distinct insuring agreements. One covers the garage operations and the other covers the non-auto loss exposures. There are separate limits of liability that apply to each and different descriptions of "Who is an insured."

Garagekeepers Coverage. — This is basically commercial bailee coverage for damage to vehicles that are in the care, custody or control of the insured.

Physical Damage Coverage. — Provides insurance for both dealers and nondealers. There are some special provisions that apply to policies issued to auto dealers. For example the Value Reporting Provision which is used to determine the physical damage premiums for a dealer's fluctuating inventory of vehicles.

MOTOR CARRIER COVERAGE FORM.

The Motor Carrier Coverage Form provides liability coverage for any person or organization that uses transportation by an auto in the operation of a commercial enterprise. The form is patterned after the Business Auto and Garage Coverage forms.

Types of organizations that would use this form include for-hire carriers of passengers or property and insureds who transport their own property or passengers by auto.

A motor carrier may be a common carrier who offers service to the general public, a contract carrier who transports goods for others under contract or a private carrier who transports its own goods in its own trucks. Owner-operators are independent contractors who use their own tractors to haul trailers provided by independent contractors or trucking firms.

PROFESSIONAL LIABILITY INSURANCE.

Professional Liability Insurance provides insurance coverage for liability loss exposures faced by professionals that is not available under the Commercial General Liability (CGL).

Those who are in need of such insurance fall into two categories. The first is "Malpractice Insurance" which provides coverage for those professions that work with the human body; i.e., medical doctors, dentists and other health care workers for loss from their professional service or from failing to do so. Also included in this category are druggists and beauticians whose work is also with the human body.

The second is "Errors and Omissions Insurance" which provides coverage for those who make decisions which can affect individuals and businesses favorably if conducted properly and unfavorably if the insured errs or omit something to the detriment of a client. Common professions in this category are accountants, lawyers, engineers, stock brokers and insurance producers.

The Professional Liability policies generally are "Claims-Made" policies and the defense costs can be outside of the policy limits. In some professions the policies permit the insured to participate in any decision to settle or not. Many of these coverages are written on a group basis where all members of a professional group can become insured under the policy. The policies also may be subject to a large deductible that would apply to each event.

Management Liability Policies. — The advent of many new regulatory rules that apply to business has caused the development of professional liability policies that are less about the acts of individuals and more about wrongful acts of an organization and its management. Examples are Directors and Officers liability and Employment Practices liability.

CHAPTER FOUR

BASIC PRINCIPLES & CONCEPTS OF OTHER IMPORTANT INSURANCE PROGRAMS

INTRODUCTION.

Several important lines of insurance will be reviewed in this chapter. These include Workers Compensation Insurance, Crime Insurance, Equipment Breakdown Insurance, Ocean Marine and Inland Marine Insurance, Umbrella and Excess Insurance, Reinsurance, Environmental Insurance and Aircraft Insurance.

WORKERS COMPENSATION & EMPLOYERS LIABILITY INSURANCE.

At the turn of the 20th century, statutes were enacted that changed the method of compensating injured workers from a voluntary or a court required award to a mandatory program of benefits for which the employer was primarily responsible. These were the Workers Compensation and Employers Liability statutes that were enacted by the various states.

There are two basic loss exposures that can affect an employer with respect to workers injured on the job. The first is the statutory Workers Compensation exposure for injury or occupational disease "arising out of or in the course of employment."

The second is the Employers Liability exposure for those individuals that are exempt from workers compensation laws but for whose injury the employer may be liable. Another employers liability loss exposure is a spouse or child who has lost the companionship of an injured worker and seeks financial recovery from the employer.

Under a workers compensation act, an injured employee loses the right to sue for common-law damages and the provisions of the act become the sole remedy for the employee. However in some states an injured worker is allowed to file suit against his or her employer if the at-work injury was caused due to the willful and wanton negligence of the employer.

The workers compensation laws impose absolute liability on the employer for an injury to a worker that arises out of or in the course of employment. The law covers most employees with the exception in some states of domestics, casual laborers and farm workers.

WORKERS COMPENSATION LAWS.

Prior to the enactment of workers compensation laws, the employee had to establish that the employer was at fault for the injury in order to seek recovery. The employer had three common law defenses to the employee's claim. They were 1) contributory negligence on the part of the employee, 2) assumed risk by the employee or 3) a fellow worker was responsible.

At that time most injured workers were unsuccessful in lawsuits against their employers. Considerable problems existed with both sides blaming the other for the cause of the injury. Because of this and social pressure, the states moved to pass the Workers Compensation Acts. The first workers compensation law that was declared constitutional was in Wisconsin in 1911.

WORKERS COMPENSATION AND EMPLOYERS LIABILITY POLICY.

Following the passage of the Workers Compensation Act in the various states the insurance industry developed an insurance policy which covered both the Workers Compensation and Employers Liability exposure.

Today the workers compensation policy is a monoline policy and it is not designed to be included within a Commercial Package Policy (CPP). It has uniform provisions even though benefits vary by state. The policy can be used in the various states without endorsement because the workers compensation law of the particular state is specifically incorporated into the contract by reference.

The standard policy form has a general section and six parts. These are Part One — Coverage for Workers Compensation, Part Two — Coverage for Employers Liability, Part Three — Other states insurance, Part Four — The duties of the insured in the event of loss, Part Five — Provisions related to the premium determination and Part Six — Policy conditions.

For an injury or disease to be covered under a workers compensation act, the following is required: 1) there must be notification to the employer, 2) there must be impairment, 3) the impairment must be caused by a covered injury or disease and 4) the impairment must be work related. Non-work related injury or disease is not covered under a workers compensation act.

WORKERS COMPENSATION BENEFITS.

The benefits available under the policy basically include all medical expenses, disability income (indemnity benefits), rehabilitation costs and death benefits. The amount paid under these benefits is established by the individual state workers compensation acts.

Medical benefits. — Benefits available are medical, hospital, surgical, and other health care costs, including physical therapy and prosthetic devices.

Disability income benefits. — The compensation for lost wages is based on a formula that involves the employee's own wages, is subject to a minimum and maximum and is a weekly benefit. The employee's temporary disability is evaluated as being either 1) total permanent disability, 2) total temporary disability, 3) partial permanent disability or 4) partial temporary disability. The ultimate indemnity benefit is based on the determined level of disability.

In most states disability income benefits are subject to a retroactive deductible. This is a waiting period which, if met, will then pay from the first day of disability. In addition disability benefits are paid for the loss of or the loss of use of body members or a restriction in the use of a body part.

Rehabilitation. — For the injured worker rehabilitation is a major goal of the workers compensation system and benefits are provided in most states.

Death benefits. — In the event of an on the job death of an employee the benefit is also based on the worker's past weekly wage and paid monthly to the surviving spouse and minor children. In addition there is a burial expense allowance.

WORKERS COMPENSATION REGULATORY RULES.

In most states there is a board or commission responsible for administering the workers compensation law. When an accident occurs the worker notifies the employer of the injury. A report is submitted to the employer's insurance company which in turn transmits it to the administrative agency.

When an employer or its insurance company does not contest the claim it is settled by agreement. The agreement is to be in compliance with the law and is subject to review by the agency.

If the employer contests a claim there would be a hearing by the administrative agency. The decision of the hearing officer may be appealed to the full board or the appropriate court.

Most employees are covered under a state Workers Compensation Act. However some states exempt or restrict certain occupations (farm labor, domestic workers, and casual employees) and may also exempt an employer with less than a stated number of employees. In some states there are occupations which may elect into or out of coverage under the law.

Workers compensation coverage may be provided for some public employees or they may have an alternative plan. Federal compensation laws cover federal employees, maritime workers and railroad workers in interstate commerce.

An individual must qualify as an employee under the law to receive benefits. An employee is defined as an individual who is hired to perform services for another under the direction and control of that party.

Independent contractors are not considered employees in most instances. However when a question arises as to the status of an individual it can be resolved by a court or administrative body.

WORKERS COMPENSATION JURISDICTION RULES.

Determining the applicable jurisdiction when an employee from one state is injured in another state depends on the law in question. Factors considered in determining the proper jurisdiction include the following: 1) the place and nature of employment, 2) the place where the employee was hired, 3) the employee's place of residence and 4) the jurisdiction of the employer's domicile.

Based on the facts of the case the claim could be filed in the state where the worker is injured, the state where the worker was hired, the state where the employee resides or the state where the employing company is located.

Federal jurisdiction is generally granted under federal legislation for specific types of employment. For example the United States Longshoremen and Harbor Workers Compensation Act provides an exclusive remedy for those covered under the Act. The injured employee would not be eligible for workers compensation benefits. While the legislation was intended to cover longshoremen and harbor workers it has been extended over the years to cover others besides those directly involved in maritime activities.

Workers Compensation Acts as established by the various states require an employer to demonstrate financial ability to pay claims. This can be done through a private insurance company, a state assigned risk plan, state funds (competitive or monopolistic) or qualified "self-insurance" plans (regulated by the states).

An "assigned risk" plan is sometimes referred to as the last resort for an applicant seeking workers compensation insurance after having been denied coverage in the private market. The applicant is "assigned" to an insurance company who issues a standard policy at what are generally higher rates than they would charge their other insureds.

COMMERCIAL CRIME INSURANCE.

Crimes are violations of the law that can be punished by a government body. The three elements of a crime loss are: 1) Items subject to loss — Money, securities and property other than money covered by the commercial crime policy, 2) Causes of loss — Employee dishonesty, money, securities, forgery and alteration, robbery, burglary, safe burglary, theft, disappearance and destruction, computer fraud, forgery and extortion and 3) Financial impact of a crime loss — Resultant loss of property taken (theft) or damaged (attempted theft).

COMMERCIAL CRIME COVERAGE PART.

The Crime Coverage Part of the Commercial Package Policy (CPP) is made up of the following sections: 1) Commercial Crime Declaration, 2) Crime General Provisions Form, 3) Crime Coverage Form(s) and 4) Any Necessary Endorsements.

The Commercial Crime program uses Crime Coverage Forms with the CPP and Crime Policy Forms when issued as a monoline policy. The difference between the two types of forms is that the former has the Common Policy Conditions form attached while the latter form contains common policy conditions.

The Crime Coverage Forms can be used to insure commercial and not-for-profit organizations other than financial institutions. There is a separate set of forms used for government bodies such as state governments and other public entities. Also available are Employee Theft and Forgery forms for organizations that only want those coverages.

There are two versions of the Coverage Forms and the Policy Forms. These are 1) the Discovery form which is used to cover losses discovered during the policy period regardless of when they occurred even if before the policy period and 2) the Loss Sustained form which only covers losses that occur during the policy period or within one year after the policy expire. The Loss Sustained forms are the most common used.

COMMERCIAL CRIME INSURING AGREEMENTS.

There are seven self-contained Loss Sustained forms with each having its individual insuring agreement. The insured selects from these forms the ones that provide the coverage that is wanted along with any applicable endorsements. The coverage provided by each of the seven Loss Sustained forms is as follows.

Employee Theft. — This form provides coverage for the employer against the theft of its property by one of its employees. Theft is defined as the unlawful taking of money, securities or other tangible property as well as forgery committed by an employee. Computer programs, electronic data and other similar property are excluded.

An employee is a natural person currently employed or who was an employee in the thirty days prior to the theft and who was paid salary, wages or commission. The individual must have been under the control and direction of the insured. Coverage territory is the United States, its territories and possessions, Puerto Rico and Canada. Any employee temporarily outside the policy territory is covered for ninety days.

Forgery or Alteration. — The insuring agreement of this form provides coverage for loss to the insured or its representatives due to the forgery or alteration of checks or similar instruments. It does not pay for loss resulting from the insured knowingly accepting items forged or altered by others.

The forgery or alteration must be made or drawn by or drawn upon the insured or by someone acting as the insured's agent or that is purported to have been so made or drawn. Coverage does not apply to dishonest acts of the insured, officers or employees. The coverage is worldwide.

Inside the Premises-Theft of Money and Securities. — Money and securities located inside a premises or banking premises are covered by this form. A "premises" is defined as the interior of an occupied commercial property while a "banking premises" is the interior of a banking institution or safe depository.

An insured loss can be caused by burglary, robbery, theft or other unlawful taking of money or securities from inside the premises. Damage to the premises is covered if the insured owns or is responsible for the property. There is coverage if a safe or similar container is damaged by safe burglary or an attempt thereto.

Money and securities that disappear or are destroyed are covered even if not caused by an unlawful act. For example a premises fire destroys currency.

Inside the Premises — Robbery or Safe Burglary of Other Property. — The definition of "robbery" involves the taking of money or other valuable goods from a custodian by force or with the threat of force. Also if an unlawful act such as shoplifting is observed by a custodian it is also deemed robber. A salesperson or cashier would be considered a custodian for coverage purposes.

Safe burglary involves taking property from a locked safe or vault including the removal of the container from inside the premises. For coverage to apply there must be evidence of forcible entry or an attempt to the container. Any damage to the premises as a result of the burglary or attempt is also covered.

Outside the Premises. — Money, securities and other property outside the premises and in the custody and care of a messenger or armored vehicle company is covered by this insuring agreement. A messenger is defined as the named insured, a relative, partner or member of the insured or any employee who has custody of the property outside the premises when the loss occurs.

Money and securities are covered against theft, disappearance or destruction while other property is covered against actual or attempted robbery. The coverage territory is the United States, its territories and possessions, Puerto Rico and Canada.

Computer Fraud. — This form covers loss of money, securities and other property caused by the fraudulent transfer of property by use of a computer inside the premises or banking premises to a person or place outside the premises. The computer involved can be on the premises, owned by the insured or by an outsider using other computer equipment on or off premises. Computer theft by an employee is not covered. The transfer can be to anywhere in the world.

Funds Transfer Fraud. — Coverage is for loss of money and securities from an insured's account at a financial institution due to "fraudulent instruction" to transfer or deliver funds. This term fraudulent instruction is defined as electronic instructions completed without the insured's consent, including forged or altered written instruction or instructions the insured received that were prepared by someone without the knowledge or consent of the insured. Computer Fraud is excluded as it is covered under the Forgery or Alteration form.

Money Orders and Counterfeit Money. — Coverage is for loss from money orders that are not paid when presented and counterfeit money that was accepted in good faith in commerce.

COMMERCIAL CRIME COVERAGE EXCLUSIONS.

These exclusions affect provisions of the various forms with some applying to all insuring agreements while others are specific to one or another insuring agreement.

General Exclusions. — On the Loss Sustained form the exclusions include 1) Acts committed by you, your partners or your members, 2) Acts of employees learned of by you prior to the policy period, 3) Acts of employees, managers, directors, trustees or representatives, 4) Confidential information, 5) Government action (seizure or destruction by order of government authority), 6) Indirect loss of business income, payment of damages, expenses incurred to establish existence or amount of loss, 7) Legal expenses (except those under forgery and alteration insuring agreement), 8) Nuclear hazard, 9) Pollution and 10) War and Military Actions.

Other Exclusions Applicable to Specific Forms. — These include Employee Theft, Inside the Premises and Outside the Premises, Computer Fraud and Funds Transfer Fraud.

COMMERCIAL CRIME COVERAGE CONDITIONS.

All of the insuring agreements are affected by policy conditions. The conditions found in the Crime Insurance forms include those found in other policies such as concealment, misrepresentation, fraud, liberalization and loss covered under more than one coverage. Others include interests insured, where coverage applies, when coverage applies, extended period to discover loss, loss sustained during prior insurance issued by us or any affiliate and loss sustained during prior insurance not issued by us or any affiliate.

COMMERCIAL CRIME COVERAGE DUTIES AFTER A LOSS.

These policy requirements following a loss include notifying the insurance company as soon as possible, notifying the police when a law has been violated, submitting to examination under oath, submitting proof of loss within 120 days, cooperating with the insurance company and retaining sufficient records to verify the extent of loss.

In a loss where money is involved it is valued at face value while securities are valued at their market value the close of the business on the day that the loss was discovered and property is valued at the cost to repair or replace.

With regard to employee theft there are conditions regarding the termination of any employee and the employee benefit plans. An employee may be terminated as soon as the insured knows of the loss. There is coverage for the loss but coverage is terminated for the employee as soon as loss is known. Coverage on any employee can be terminated with thirty days notice. With respect to the employee benefit plans this condition eliminates the need to attach the ERISA compliance endorsement.

FINANCIAL INSTITUTION BONDS.

Needs of a financial institution to cover its unique crime loss exposures are met by the financial institution bond. While it is an insurance policy it is referred to as a bond since it also covers employee dishonesty which has been referred to as a fidelity bond.

Organizations needing such coverage include banks, savings and loan firms, credit unions, stock brokers, finance and insurance companies. If the firm is eligible for a financial institution bond it is not eligible for the crime insurance program. Forms used are prepared by the Surety and Fidelity Association of America (SFAA), and ISO as well as some insurance companies. In the past this type of coverage was referred to as a "Bankers Blanket bond."

SURETYSHIP.

Suretyship is not insurance. It is a guaranty agreement involving three parties—the principal (obligor), the obligee and the surety (guarantor). As an example the principal is a contractor who needs a performance bond to cover a new job. The obligee is the owner of the property where the job will be performed and who wants the principal to have a bond. The surety, after checking on the experience and financial condition of the principal, issues the performance bond requested by the owner (obligee). There is no room in the surety bond premium for losses. The surety would not issue a bond if a loss were anticipated. When there is a default (loss) and the bond is paid the surety can take legal action against the principal to recover the amount paid.

There are many types of surety bonds. Some are used in matters involving contractual obligations such as bid bonds, performance bonds and maintenance bonds. Other bonds are used in matters involving legal and statutory obligations such as license and permit bonds and public official bonds. Court bonds include appeal bonds, replevin bonds and fiduciary bonds. There are also miscellaneous bonds used for various personal and unique business situations.

EQUIPMENT BREAKDOWN INSURANCE

For many years this coverage was called Boiler and Machinery Insurance. However with the addition of many types of machinery and electrical equipment to the policy it was revised and issued as the Equipment Breakdown Protection Coverage Form.

Equipment Breakdown coverage is an important commercial coverage but needs to be used in connection with Commercial Property Insurance and Commercial Liability Insurance in order to fully protect the insured in the event of a major explosion, mechanical or electrical breakdown.

Commercial property insurance policies do not provide coverage for loss caused by mechanical breakdown, electrical breakdown or steam boiler explosions that involves equipment and the property around it. The Equipment Breakdown policy provides insurance against such loss to covered property as well as to the covered equipment itself.

Commercial liability insurance would provide protection in the event the explosion or breakdown caused bodily injury or property damage to a third-party.

EQUIPMENT BREAKDOWN INSURING AGREEMENTS

The Equipment Breakdown form contains ten insuring agreements. The insured selects from the insuring agreements and premium is paid for those chosen. Some are basic coverages while others are coverage extensions.

The cause of loss covered in the Equipment Breakdown form is the "breakdown" of "covered equipment." Breakdown is defined as the direct physical loss that causes damage to covered equipment and results in the repair or replacement of that equipment as a result of one of the covered malfunctions. These are 1) the failure of pressure or vacuum equipment, 2) mechanical failure, including rupturing or bursting caused by centrifugal force and 3) electrical failure including arcing.

The definition of "covered equipment" is broad and includes 1) Equipment built to operate under internal pressure or vacuum, 2) Electrical or mechanical equipment used in the generation, transmission or utilization of energy and 3) Communication and computer equipment.

Exclusions that apply to the definition of breakdown include such conditions as defects, leakage, computer viruses, damage to vacuum or gas tubes and damage to foundations or support structures.

Excluded property under the form includes computer media, vehicles, aircraft, watercraft, excavation or construction equipment, parts and tools subject to periodic replacement, medical diagnostic equipment and equipment manufactured by the insured for sale.

There are ten insuring agreements. The three major ones are 1) property damage, 2) expediting expenses and 3) business income and/or extra expense. The remaining seven insuring agreements are available for insureds with specific business risk protection needs. They are 4) spoilage damage, 5) utility interruption, 6) newly acquired premises, 7) ordinance or law, 8) errors and omissions, 9) brands and labels and 10) contingent business income and extra expense.

Property Damage. — The insurance company agrees to pay for direct damage to "covered property" which is defined as property that is owned by or is in the care, custody and control of the insured for which the insured is legally liable. This definition is broader that that of "covered equipment" and both must be at the described location.

Equipment breakdown insurance covers damage to the covered equipment but also damage to other property as a result of the damage to covered equipment. Debris removal is included under this insuring agreement.

Expediting Expenses. — Coverage is provided for reasonable extra expenses needed to make temporary repairs or to obtain necessary parts quickly to expedite repairs.

Business Income and Extra Expense. — An equipment breakdown causing damage to both covered equipment and covered property can create a loss of business income and extra expense for the insured. The coverage can be for both business income and extra expense or only for extra expense. The insured can cover its own operations as well as those at a dependant supplier's facility.

EQUIPMENT BREAKDOWN FORM CONDITIONS.

The conditions found in the equipment breakdown form are generally the same as in other property insurance policies. However there are three that are specific to the policy.

Suspension. — This condition allows an insurance company to suspend coverage on a covered item that it considers to be at risk due to its condition or situation. The action can be taken immediately by an insurance company inspector on site or an insurance company may send a written notice if it learns that an insured has failed or refused to take action when advised of a potentially serious problem. The suspension can only be lifted by endorsing the policy to provide coverage on a particular item.

Joint or Disputed Loss Agreement. — When an insured has equipment breakdown coverage with one insurance company and commercial property coverage with another there may be disputes as to how a claim involving both policies should be settled. If the policies have this agreement then the manner in which an insured can ask the settlement to be made is that each insurance company pays its own loss and one-half of the disputed amounts.

Jurisdictional Inspections. — Many governmental agencies will require that boilers and pressure vessels be inspected by qualified inspector. Most inspectors employed by insurance companies are licensed and can perform these "jurisdictional" inspections for their clients.

MARINE INSURANCE.

The field of Marine insurance has historically been divided into Ocean Marine (Wet) and Inland Marine (Dry) insurance. The oldest insurance line is Ocean Marine and provided protection for ships and their cargo as they transited the oceans from port to port. Inland Marine developed later as goods moving inland from the coasts had need for insurance coverages as well.

OCEAN MARINE INSURANCE.

Ocean Marine insurance is one of the more fascinating areas of the insurance business since it dates back to historical times. Probably the most famous of the early marine insurance underwriters were those at Mr. Lloyd's coffee house in the 18th century which was the forerunner of Lloyd's, London a world famous insurance exchange.

Their operations continue today as the syndicates at Lloyd's underwrite worldwide ocean marine insurance as well as insurance coverages for nearly all types of loss exposures on land, sea or in the air. While ocean marine insurance is a specialty line there are many insurance companies involved in underwriting ocean marine risks.

Ocean Marine policy. — The policy provides for three major classes of coverages which are 1) Hull Insurance — The physical damage coverage for damage to the vessel, 2) Cargo Insurance — Coverage is provided for goods which are carried by the vessel from port to port. The cargo may be owned by the ship owner or by the buyer or seller of the goods and 3) Protection and Indemnity Insurance — This is liability coverage for the ship owner and the operations of the vessel. It is similar to other forms of liability insurance.

An Ocean Marine contract continues to utilize some of the very old styles of language that have been used from the beginning. For example some of the perils covered are rovers, assailing thieves, barratry of the master and acts of princes or kings. It is interesting that this wording has not changed in centuries of use.

However in the same contract, there is reference to nuclear warfare which brings the contract up to date. The reason for the wording not changing is that many of the terms and words have been agreed upon by American, English and International maritime courts of law and because of this the underwriters are hesitant to change them.

INLAND MARINE INSURANCE.

The need for Inland Marine insurance developed as commerce began to move goods inland from the sea. Such coverage would expand to eventually involve networks and instrumentalities of transportation as this field of insurance grew.

The transportation networks involve trucks and trains and the instrumentalities are bridges and tunnels. Much of the terminology of this coverage is borrowed from the Ocean marine contract but it also has a close relationship to many of the property insurance coverages.

UNDERWRITING INLAND MARINE POLICIES.

The field of Inland Marine insurance is extremely versatile. It is used to cover property and goods that tend to move about or have an element of transportation or communications involved and often are small and of high value. Examples are furs, jewelry, art, camera equipment, and musical instruments as well as construction equipment and tools. Coverage under an inland marine policy is generally worldwide.

The categories of property that can be insured under inland marine forms are stated in The Nation-wide Marine Definition. These are 1) imports, 2) exports and domestic shipments, 3) instrumentalities of transportation and communication, 4) personal property floaters and 5) commercial property floaters.

COVERAGE UNDER INLAND MARINE POLICIES.

There are two approaches to coverage when underwriting an Inland Marine policy. One is specified perils coverage where the covered causes of loss such as fire or theft are stated. The other which is more common is an all risks form where all causes of loss except those specifically excluded are covered.

There are both nonfiled and filed inland marine policies. The former are used for risks where a standard form would be impractical. The latter uses standard forms and class rates.

The classes of filed commercial inland marine policies include: 1) accounts receivable, 2) camera and musical instrument dealers, 3) film, 4) floor plan merchandise, 5) implement and equipment dealers, 6) jewelry dealers, 7) mail, 8) musical instruments, 9) photographic equipment, 10) physicians equipment, 11) signs, 12) theatrical property and 13) valuable papers and records.

UMBRELLA INSURANCE, EXCESS INSURANCE AND REINSURANCE.

There are times in both Personal and Commercial insurance programs where the insured wishes to have higher limits and/or broader coverages than are available on the basic insurance policies. This need can be solved using an Umbrella insurance policy or Excess insurance coverage.

Reinsurance is used by insurance companies to reduce the amount of loss exposure insured by moving some of it to a reinsurance company. It also serves as a method of strengthening the financial position of the insurance company.

UMBRELLA INSURANCE.

An Umbrella insurance policy is available for both Personal and Commercial insurance programs. The Umbrella policy is designed to "sit on top" of required underlying policies. In the case of a Personal Umbrella policy the underlying policies could be a Personal Auto policy and a Homeowners program policy selected by the insured.

The umbrella policy can provide additional coverage over the per occurrence limit of the underlying liability policy as well as over the per aggregate limit. It also may provide coverage with a deductible for a liability claim not covered by one of the underlying policies. The underlying coverages must be maintained in order for the Umbrella coverage to apply.

If a personal umbrella policy is written with a $1 million limit and the Auto policy has a Combined Single Liability limit of $250,000 the insured would be protected up to $1,250,000 if held legally liable for an auto accident (subject to all provisions, conditions and exclusions of the underlying policy).

One caveat, the Uninsured and Underinsured liability coverages are often excluded on an Umbrella policy. An insured should verify this to be certain the coverage applies.

EXCESS INSURANCE.

Excess insurance is used primarily in commercial insurance programs. It provides additional dollar amounts of insurance over the primary policies. It can also be "stacked" in layers of insurance provided to the same insured. Excess insurance is used with both property and liability programs.

For example, an insured has an underlying insurance policy with limits of $1 million. In order to increase the total coverage to $5 million an excess liability policy is purchased with a $4 million limit.

Some excess insurance policies may be written to cover a specific underlying coverage. One example would be to issue an excess policy over Products

Liability only. This policy can be written as a self-contained policy subject to its own terms.

Another approach is for the excess policy to be a "following form" policy. This means that the coverage provided by the excess policy is identical to the underlying policy with respect to provisions, conditions and exclusions.

An excess policy can also be written as a combination of a self-contained and a following form. This would be done by issuing s following form policy and then modifying it by endorsement to restrict or eliminate coverage for a particular loss exposure.

If a very large amount of insurance is required above the primary policy there may be several layers of insurance in forces such as a $1 million layer then a $5 million layer topped by a $20 million layer and then another $40 million layer which is split 25/75 with one excess policy being for $10 million and the other for $30 million. This would give the insured a total of $66 million in coverage.

REINSURANCE.

The Reinsurer is often referred to as an "insurance company's insurance company." What takes place is that a reinsurer agrees to pay claims that are greater than the primary policy's limit of insurance.

In most cases the reinsurance policy is written to cover a number of primary policies. For example, an insurance company writes primary automobile insurance on a large group of customers. If the total losses for that group of policies exceed a pre-set dollar amount the reinsurer will pay the excess amount to the insurance company.

Reinsurance is also used by an insurance company to expand is ability to meet financial needs in marketing and expansion of its underwriting. This is accomplished by moving some of its committed loss exposures to the reinsurer.

The insurance company pays the reinsurer a premium for the coverage. If a reinsurer seeks to have its business insured that transaction is called "retrocession." The transaction by the reinsurer is called "ceding" the loss exposure to the retrocessioner.

ENVIRONMENTAL INSURANCE.

The limited environmental insurance provided under the commercial property and liability insurance policies in an insured's program may prove to be inadequate and additional coverage is desired.

The available environment insurance policies are many and varied rather than standard policies. Some of the types of environmental policies are 1) Site specific environmental impairment, 2) Underground storage tank coverage, 3) Remediation, 4) Contractors pollution and 5) Environmental professional's errors and omissions.

Since environmental coverages are not standard the provisions and exclusions can be modified and endorsed to basically tailor make the policy to fit the expected needs of the insured. Policies may cover either sudden or gradual release of pollutants, coverage for clean-up costs, defense costs and proof of financial responsibility.

AIRCRAFT INSURANCE.

There are several categories of aircraft which enter into the underwriting of an aircraft policy. Basically the liability insurance resembles an auto policy as it pays for the legal liability of an insured arising out of the ownership, maintenance and or use of the aircraft. There is also Hull coverage available which is the physical damage coverage for the aircraft.

The categories of aircraft are Airline, Business and Pleasure, Industrial Aid, Commercial Use, Special Use, Instruction and Rental, and Sales Demonstration.

The Industrial Aid category involves corporate owned aircraft transporting staff and flown by professional pilots. Commercial Use is for charter operators and other profit seeking operators. Special Use would include crop dusters and police patrols.

Underwriting aircraft insurance includes not only the airplane and its use but the qualifications of those individuals who will be flying the plane. The exclusions are similar to other liability policies.

Other coverages include Medical Payments insurance, nonowned aircraft liability and passenger voluntary settlement coverage. The last which is used in connection with industrial aid aircraft is also known as admitted liability coverage and provides a scheduled benefit if a passenger suffers death, dismemberment or loss of sight.

CHAPTER FIVE

BASIC PRINCIPLES & CONCEPTS OF RISK MANAGEMENT

INTRODUCTION.

In the insurance industry the term Risk Management has become commonly used to describe a program which includes the use of insurance and other alternative techniques to protect an individual or organization from economic loss. Underlying the risk management concept is that various techniques other than insurance can be used to help reduce both premium costs and potential losses.

As used here the term "risk" means the uncertainty that an economic loss will occur. There are two kinds of risk that are faced by an individual or organization. These are static (pure) risk and dynamic (speculative) risk.

Static risk. — This form of risk exists if a person or organization can only suffer a loss. For example a building burns to the ground. Even though insurance may pay to rebuild the structure the insured has still lost the amount of the premium. Only static risks are insurable and can be treated by the risk management process.

Dynamic risk. — This form of risk involves the chance of either a gain or a loss. The entrepreneur faces dynamic risk in bringing a new product to market. It may be a success (gain) or a failure (loss). Such dynamic risk is not insurable.

RISK MANAGEMENT PRINCIPLES AND CONCEPTS.

Risk management involves a formal decision making process. The goal of this process is to reduce or eliminate the chance of economic loss from static risks. The development of the risk management approach has led to the formation of basic principles and concepts to use in the process.

The person who undertakes the establishment of the program is called a risk manager.

DEVELOPING A RISK MANAGEMENT PROGRAM.

Risk Management programs can be used by commercial organization or by an individual or family, An effective risk management program involves identifying the risks, considering alternative techniques, selecting the best technique, implementing the program and evaluating the results. The evaluation is needed to determine if the program is working or needs to be revised.

Identifying the risks. — Here the risk manager has to seek out and assemble information about the organization and its various exposures to loss. Initially this can be a lengthy process as it involves collecting considerable date about the organization not only current but past and future expected activities.

Information review. — It is important for the risk manager to determine the various factors involved in the organization. There are three questions to be answered.

"Who are we?" — Information is needed on the history of the company, its various entities, ownership, officers, directors and management. For many organizations it is necessary and important to consider past, present and potential future loss exposures. As an example actions or activities by a predecessor company or official could cause litigation to occur today. It is particularly important to review all mergers and acquisitions even if a unit may no longer be part of the organization.

"Where are we?" — Next the risk manager must determine the locations of all real estate and personal property. Again, past, present and future locations should be reviewed. There are some federal and state regulations today that can hold a current or even a former owner of property responsible under the regulation for prior activities.

"What are we?" — Finally the risk manager considers the various operations and products of the organization past, present and future. Current operations and products should be able to be easily reviewed. The risk management concerns for future activities and products should be considered company wide. It is necessary to review earlier and former operations and products as well. For example a product that was marketed by the company or its predecessor years earlier and no longer available could still become the subject of current litigation.

The answers to these three questions regarding entities, locations and operations are fundamental to the success of the risk management program as they aid in determining the static risks faced by the firm past, present and future. This also develops information that may be necessary for insurance applications. Past history is important as well as future plans because of the affect both may have on developing the risk management program and the underwriting of any insurance programs.

Inspection and Review. — This is the second step in the identification process. "Inspection" involves a physical tour of the facilities to look for potential loss exposures. "Review" means to study documents and records to try to locate potential loss exposures. While time consuming it is both necessary and important for the risk manager to conduct a thorough investigation using both methods.

There are four groups of loss exposures to identify and to review. These are the following:

Liability loss exposures. — People, things and activities that can injury other people or their property.

Property loss exposures. — Real or personal property that can be damaged, destroyed or disappear.

Net income loss exposures. — These involve the loss of a firm's income or profits that could occur because its property was damaged, destroyed or disappeared. Liability loss exposures can also affect the net income of the organization.

Personnel loss exposures. — Conditions which can cause harm to employees and result in a loss to the firm. Examples are death, disability and disease which directly affect a key person or operation in the organization.

Analyzing the information obtained. — The next step in the development of a risk management program is to analyze the loss exposures and other information that has been accumulated during the identification, inspection and review stages in order to determine how the overall loss exposures can best be treated.

A major factor in the analysis of loss exposures is to consider alternative techniques to use to treat them other than simply purchasing insurance products. In this stage each of the loss exposures has to be considered with respect to the frequency with which loss can occurs and the severity of a potential loss.

The basic rule about frequent losses is that they are normally small dollar losses. They are the types that become more of a nuisance than anything else. An example would be frequent cuts to employees in a sheet metal plant. Often there are loss control steps that can be taken to eliminate or reduce the problem of frequent losses.

A severe loss is usually a rare event but one with a high dollar value. These are the unexpected, unintended and often unusual losses. For example an explosion involving a major portion of a plant would be considered a severe loss.

Potential losses must also be analyzed with respect to the duration of the downtime that would be created by the loss. Some facilities and equipment can be replaced quickly while others may require considerable time to get them back operational.

Finally during the analysis stage, the risk manager must determine the limits of liability desired for liability exposures and the amount of insurance that would be needed for property, earnings and personnel loss exposures.

Selecting the best risk management technique. — The information that has been obtained by the risk manager must now be reviewed to determine which risk management techniques will be used. Some techniques are used alone while some may be used along with another technique.

There are four risk management techniques that are available to the risk manager in the development of the program. The first is avoidance which is used alone. The other three control, retention and transfer may be combined or used individually.

Avoidance. — An individual or firm can avoid a particular loss exposure by never having it or by eliminating it. For example never owning a corporate aircraft or closing an in-plant spray paint operation are examples of risk avoidance.

Control. — This technique is designed to control the hazards that can increase the chance of loss. There are two major areas of control which are property preservation and personnel conservation. The loss control activities used in both areas are 1) Loss prevention—Actions taken before a loss, 2) Loss reduction—Actions taken during or after the loss and 3) Loss analysis—Activities undertaken following the loss.

Retention. — This technique requires the firm to absorb part of the chance of economic loss. The anticipated cost of loss is intentionally retained when it is determined that the firm can absorb a particular dollar level of loss. Types of retentions are non-insurance, deductibles and percentage participations. Unfortunately risk can also be retained through ignorance when the risk manager fails to identify a particular loss exposure and no risk management technique is applied.

Transfer. — A risk of economic loss that could be caused by a particular loss exposure can be transferred to another party through a provision in a contract. A hold harmless agreement is an example where a contractor assumes the liability of a building owner for any loss that might occur while the contractor is working on the building.

Another and more common type of transfer is to a professional risk bearer—an insurance company. By purchasing an insurance policy, the risk manager transfers the chance of economic loss. In many instances when an insurance contract is purchased, there may be a requirement that the insured retain some of the risk and the insurance company may initiate or participate in loss control activities designed to reduce the chance of loss.

Implementing. — When first considered the implementation of a risk management program seems to offer little problem. However in reality there must first be management approval for the program. Second the risk manager, a staff person, must convince the line managers that the program will be beneficial for them.

In most organizations the risk manager is in a staff position located within the financial area. The risk management program to be successful must be implemented throughout the firm. There are questions as to who pays for the various parts of the program and how much time can be taken from the workers in order to educate them in the program particularly the loss control features. The full support of top management is necessary if the program is to succeed.

Monitoring. — Once the program is in place, the risk manager must monitor and evaluate its performance on a continuous basis. Monitoring can be done through inspection and loss reports received from the insurance companies as well as through reviews and other internal reports. The evaluation of the program may lead to minor revisions, which can make it even more productive.

The risk management process involves bringing together many activities to increase the probability that the firm will not suffer economic loss due to its static risks. It requires careful and deliberate study and actions on the part of the risk manager, cooperation from management and all other departments and a continuous monitoring and evaluation. When properly carried out a risk management program can result in fewer and less costly losses and reduce overall insurance costs.

SUCCESS OF A RISK MANAGEMENT PROGRAM.

As with any management program the success comes from having the workers, the supervisors and the managers all to believe in the program and work to make it a success.

Any program that is new to an organization can be met with suspicion and resentment because for some it means a change in habits while for others it may be considered to be an interference with their authority.

Top management must be prepared to support a risk management program both financially and as an organizational goal to which all employees must fully participate. Anything less not only limits the effectiveness of the program but may well end it very quickly.

CHAPTER SIX

BASIC PRINCIPLES & CONCEPTS OF LIFE INSURANCE

INTRODUCTION.

Life insurance is an important part of the insurance program of an individual, family or organization. Life insurance products can be effectively used to protect the assets and liabilities of an individual or family as well as provide a way to accumulate funds for retirement and estate planning. A basic knowledge of life insurance products is important for individuals and families.

Concerns over the need for life insurance are discussed here as well as the types of policies available and common provisions and riders. Life insurance underwriting and group life insurance also are examined.

WHY LIFE INSURANCE?

A life insurance policy is not a contract of indemnity but is a valued policy that pays a named beneficiary a stated sum upon the death of the insured. The event insured is "an uncertain time of death."

Death is premature if it occurs during an individual's economic productive period. In such cases there often are unfulfilled and unexpected financial commitments that must be met. These expenses would fall upon the survivors if proper financial planning were not in place.

Premature death creates at least four costs that may have to be met by the survivors. First, there is the termination of the worker's income and the family's share of that income. Second, there can be terminal expenses incurred that must be met such as medical bills and funeral expenses. There may also be a potential cost to society if the lack of income would force dependents into a welfare program. Finally, there are noneconomic costs such as the emotional loss of the guidance and counsel of the deceased.

Life insurance can be used to provide the funds to meet such economic needs. However, the dollar amount of life insurance necessary depends upon individual circumstances and the stage of life at which death might occur. Because of this a life insurance program should be subject to frequent review.

A life insurance program can be justified to help offset these costs because of the lost earning capacity of the deceased which was the primary financial support of these dependents.

DETERMINING THE AMOUNT OF LIFE INSURANCE.

The amount of life insurance an individual can purchase depends on his or her ability to pay the premiums and the agreement of an insurance company to provide the coverage.

It is not easy to determine the amount of life insurance that would be beneficial in the event of the premature death of an individual who financially supports a family or wishes to bequest something to others.

Individuals and families have different needs and desires to fulfill in such circumstances. One method used to help determine the amount of life insurance to have is called the "needs approach." The expected financial needs of the survivors are estimated. Social Security survivor benefits, current life insurance and other current and anticipated assets are also estimated. The aggregate amount of expected assets is then subtracted from the anticipated financial needs of the survivors to determine the additional amount of life insurance required to cover all of these projected needs.

Basic family needs include the following: 1) Estate settlement fund — Final expenses, taxes, legal fees. 2) Income for the readjustment period — Adapting to the forced lifestyle, 3) Income for the dependency period — Until the last child reaches 18 years of age, 4) Income for the "blackout period" — Period of time between being a survivor with children to being a survivor at age 60, 5) Special needs — Emergency Fund, Mortgage Payoff, Educational Needs and 6) Retirement fund — For the surviving spouse.

When estimating the amount of life insurance needed, consideration must be given to both future inflation and expected interest rates. The "needs approach" requires frequent review as the various factors can change rapidly over time as children grow, new jobs are taken, housing requirements change, educations are completed and other life style situations occur.

TYPES OF LIFE INSURANCE POLICIES.

The three basic types of life insurance are term insurance, whole life insurance and endowment insurance. A life insurance company may combine features from these basic forms into a policy specifically designed to meet the expected needs of the market.

When reviewing a life insurance product to purchase, an applicant should make certain that the producer identifies the type of policy that is the basis for the coverage offered and what additional features may have been added for the presentation.

Term life insurance. — The two basic characteristics of term insurance are 1) it is only temporary protection because coverage terminates at the end of the policy term and 2) there is no cash value or savings element.

Term life insurance is less costly than either whole life or endowment contracts. It is often used to provide financial protection for a specific period of time when the loss of the insured would create a serious financial problem for the survivors. For example, a five-year term policy on the father covering the years a child is in college.

There are several types of term life insurance policies that have different and specific uses:

Straight or Level Term. — Policy is in force for a limited period of time with the same annual premium.

Renewable Term. — Can be renewed for additional periods without evidence of insurability. Premiums will probably increase when renewed.

Convertible Term. — May be exchanged for permanent life insurance at times stated in the policy with no evidence of insurability.

Increasing Term. — The face value increases at stated times during the policy term.

Decreasing Term. — The face value decreases at stated times during the policy year. For example it could be used to pay off a mortgage upon the death of the insured.

Reentry Term. — Premiums are based on a low rate schedule but insured must periodically demonstrate evidence of insurability.

Frequently a term policy can be presented that combines some of the other types of term policies such as a level term policy that is both renewable and convertible.

Whole life insurance. — This form of life insurance has a level premium and provides lifetime protection. The two basic types are ordinary life and limited pay life insurance.

Ordinary life insurance. — This form has a level premium which is paid from the date purchased until death or age 100 when the face amount is paid to the policyholder.

Limited payment life insurance. — This is a form of whole life insurance. The premiums are level but are paid only for a stated number of years. Typical plans are 1) single pay life, 2) twenty pay life and 3) life paid up at age sixty-five. The fewer number of years that premiums are paid the higher will be the annual premium payment.

Limited payment life insurance is more popular than an ordinary life policy. A feature used today is a limited payment life policy that requires premiums to be paid for only a few years and then the premiums are paid from the interest earned on the cash reserve and/or by borrowing from the cash reserve.

Endowment insurance. — Endowment policies pay the face value to the named beneficiary if the insured would die prior to a stated date. If the insured lives beyond that date the policy proceeds are paid out to the policyholder as monthly income.

"Hybrid" types of life insurance policies. — These are policy forms, which are designed for particular needs or groups. These policies may use features from both term life and whole life insurance in their construction and have features that may modify premium, face amount, policy reserves, loan values and procedures.

Universal life insurance. — This policy has a flexible premium deposit fund that is combined with monthly renewable term insurance. The initial premium less administrative expenses is credited to the premium deposit fund and becomes the policy's initial cash value. Depending on the plan premium payments may be flexible.

Monthly a mortality charge is deducted from the premium deposit fund to purchase the pure term insurance protection. The remaining cash value is credited with a current rate of interest. Because of its design, universal life insurance can be viewed as a combination of a savings plan that earns interest and low cost renewable term insurance.

An annual disclosure statement is required to be provided to the insured which shows the amount used to purchase pure protection, the increase in savings and the administrative charges. The policy has a guaranteed minimum rate of interest paid on the cash value stated in the policy. With some policies an excess rate of interest may be paid.

The policies have considerable flexibility depending on the plan. Premiums may be increased or decreased or not paid if the cash value will cover mortality costs and expenses. The death benefit may be increased or decreased. Policy loans and cash withdrawals may be permitted based on policy provisions. The death benefit may be reduced by the amount of a withdrawal. Some policies have a surrender charge for cash withdrawal.

Variable life insurance. — Under this policy form, the face amount of insurance varies based on the investment experience of a separate account maintained by the insurance company. Premiums are invested in equities or similar investments. If the investment experience is favorable the face amount of insurance is increased. If it is unfavorable the face amount is decreased but never less than the original face amount.

Variable-Universal life insurance. — This policy has features of both variable and universal life insurance. It combines the flexibility of the universal life policy with the opportunity to select the type of investment to be used. If the investment goes well the value increases but if it does not then the value declines.

The basic characteristics of this type of policy are those of a universal life policy with two major differences. First, there is no guarantee on the accumulation of cash value as it is determined by a separate account held by the insurance company. Second, the policy owner selects the type of separate investment account desired. For example: stocks, bonds, fixed income or other type of investment.

Adjustable life insurance. — This whole life policy permits changes to the amount of life insurance, period of protection, amount of premium, and duration of the premium-paying period. It is also called "life cycle" insurance since changes in the policy can be used to conform to different periods in an insured's life.

Modified life insurance. — This is a whole life policy with premiums that are reduced for an initial period of time (three to five years) and then increased after that. It can be used by an insured that expects to have a higher income at a later date but needs coverage today. The approach used can vary. One method is to use a term policy for the first few years that automatically converts into an ordinary life policy. A second approach is to redistribute the premiums by charging a low initial premium, which is increased each year for five years and then remains level thereafter.

The Family policy. — This policy insures all family members under a single contract. It is generally sold in units that are based on the amount of insurance for the head of the family. For example, a unit can consist of $5000 of ordinary life insurance on the insured, $2000 of term insurance to age sixty-five on the spouse and $1,000 of term insurance on each child to a stated age which then usually can be converted to a whole life policy. Coverage is provided based on a single premium for all of the family members. Coverage may also be provided for any future newborn children as well.

UNDERWRITING LIFE INSURANCE.

There are three parties in the life insurance transaction. These are the insured, the beneficiary and the owner. The latter is the one that has control over the policy and can change the beneficiary or borrow against the policy reserve. The owner can be the insured or the beneficiary or a third-party such as a trustee or employer.

It is also important to note that in order for an individual or organization to purchase a life insurance policy, the buyer must have an "insurable interest" in the person to be insured. For example, a spouse, an employer, or a third party who would suffer a financial loss if the insured dies.

The underwriting activities used for life insurance can vary based on 1) the type of policy, 2) the age of the applicant, 3) the amount of insurance requested and 4) the responses given on a written application which is attached to and becomes a part of the insurance contract.

The application is a very important document which must be completed accurately and completely. It must be read and understood by the applicant and signed in the presence of the producer. An incomplete application can cause delay in obtaining the policy or even declination by the underwriter. The completed application is attached to and becomes a part of the life insurance contract. Any false or misleading statement made by the applicant on the application can be used to void the policy.

The underwriting objective is to develop a profitable and growing book of business for the life insurance company. A life underwriter attempts to issue coverage for a group of insureds who have an expected mortality rate the same as or lower than that for the population as a whole. If successful the insurance company can avoid the consequences of "adverse selection."

Life insurance company loss experience has shown that to predict expected mortality rates the following underwriting factors are important: Age, Sex, Health, Occupation, Personal habits, Foreign residence or recent immigration

Based on the information obtained from the applicant and other sources the life insurance underwriter can take one of three actions. The applicant may be rated "standard" and charged the basic premium. The applicant may be considered "substandard" and charged a higher premium. Finally, the applicant can be declined because the chance of loss is too great. Some life insurance companies identify preferred risks for which they provide a premium that is lower than the standard premium.

In addition to an application form the life insurance company will request a medical history form be completed. Depending on a number of factors such as age or amount of insurance requested a limited or full physical examination may be required. There may also be a questionnaire covering social habits, occupation and other similar topics which the underwriter reviews during the underwriting process.

Other sources of information on the applicant which may be used, include a report from the Medical Information Bureau (MIB) that collects information on individuals who are denied life insurance, medical records from the applicant's personal physician and in some cases a credit report.

OPTIONS AND BENEFITS FOR POLICYHOLDERS.

Whole life insurance policies and some interest sensitive life policies have various options and benefits available to the insured during his or her lifetime. These features have to do with policy reserves, premiums and dividends. The owner of the policy is the party that has control over these matters.

Options and benefits dealing with policy reserves include the nonforfeiture options which are 1) Extended term insurance, 2) Paid-up insurance values, 3) Cash value and 4) Policy loan value.

Options and benefits regarding premiums and changes in coverage and insurability are 1) Grace period, 2) Automatic premium loan, 3) Reinstatement provision, 4) Policy change provision and 5) Guaranteed insurability provision.

Options and benefits with regard to dividends. — A policy that pays dividends is called a "participating" policy while one that does not pay dividends is a "nonparticipating" policy. Dividends are not guaranteed. They can be paid in cash or credited to the next premium payment. Dividends also can be used to purchase paid-up additions which are single premium amounts of paid-up insurance. Another method is to accumulate the dividends at interest to be added to the death benefit.

TAX TREATMENT OF LIFE INSURANCE PREMIUMS AND PROCEEDS.

The taxation of insurance policy features is primarily a function of the federal government however individual states may treat these funds differently and should be determined locally. Because tax laws and regulations change frequently it is important that your tax advisor address any questions on this matter.

Individual life insurance. — The premiums paid by an individual for life insurance are not tax deductible. However, the proceeds of a life insurance policy are not taxed when taken in a lump sum. If they are left with the insurance company under some distribution plan any interest earned is taxable.

Group life insurance. — Group life insurance premiums are tax deductible for the employer but only for the first $50,000 of coverage. Any premiums paid for an amount over $50,000 would be taxable to the employee as income. Group life insurance proceeds are not taxable except as noted above for any interest earned.

Modified endowment contracts (MEC). — Prior to the passage of the Technical and Miscellaneous Revenue Act (TAMRA) in 1988, single premium whole life insurance policies had been sold as tax shelters since their investment earnings were nontaxable and the policy owner could borrow them without paying income tax.

Due to the provisions of TAMRA, any whole life insurance policy issued after June 20, 1988 is called a Modified Endowment Contract (MEC) and has lost many of the tax advantages that earlier policies still retain. Changes in the policy or withdrawal of funds that do not pass the IRS's seven-pay test are subject to a ten-percent tax penalty if the insured is under age 59 1/2.

GROUP LIFE INSURANCE.

In addition to individual life insurance policies many families depend on employer provided group life insurance for financial protection. The amount of group life insurance is limited by the employer and provides coverage during employment. An employee who terminates employment may convert this coverage within a stated period of time without evidence of insurability but not at the group premium rate. Retirees may be provided a reduced amount of life insurance which may be for a limited time period.

The major differences between individual and group life insurance relate to the marketing, underwriting and administration of the group insurance plans. In underwriting group insurance consideration is given to characteristics such as the age and sex distribution of the group of persons to be insured rather than the individuals in the group.

The policy owner of a group insurance contract such as an employer holds the master contract. Employees have certain rights under the contract and receive a certificate of insurance rather than a policy.

CREDIT LIFE INSURANCE.

This is a form of life insurance that is used to pay a debt if the insured dies with a balance due. Businesses that sell generally big ticket items such as autos, jewelry and furniture will offer credit life coverage to their customers. The full premium for the credit life insurance is added into the installment contract at the time of purchase. If the insured dies the balance on the account will be paid by the insurance company. There is also Disability Credit Insurance available.

ANNUITY CONTRACTS.

Another of the contracts issued by life insurance companies is the annuity contract. This is not a life insurance policy but is designed to provide regular income payments to the policyholder, called an annuitant.

Annuities differ from life insurance. — An annuity is used to spread invested capital and the interest it earns over a stated period such as the lifetime of the annuitant. Actuarial tables are used to determine how much must be paid into the contact to provide the stated benefit.

These benefits begin on a specific date and can continue until the death of the annuitant or a specific date in the future. When the annuitant dies, under some annuities, the remaining funds pass to a beneficiary.

With some annuities these payments continue for the lifetime of the annuitant even if all the paid-in funds and interest are consumed. In such cases the annuity contract eliminates considerable financial risk for the annuitant.

Underwriting annuities. — A major underwriting difference between life insurance and annuity contracts is important. With life insurance the benefits are paid when the insured dies so that the age and health of the insured is important to the underwriter. However the health of the annuity holder is not a factor in the underwriting review for an annuity since the benefits under a life annuity contract cease at the annuitant's death.

CLASSIFICATION OF ANNUITIES.

The basis for classification of annuities involves several characteristics. These include the payment plan, the date of the first benefit, the duration of the benefits, the number of lives to receive benefits and the source of annuity income.

Annuity premium payment plans. — There are two premium payment plans. The first is a single premium plan where the annuitant deposits a lump sum of money into the plan. The second is an installment premium plan where the annuitant makes regular premium payments over a period of time. Under this plan the annuitant pays from inception until the date the benefits begin.

A modified installment plan is the flexible premium plan where the annuitant can make premium payments as frequently as desired in any dollar amount. This plan is often used to build a retirement program for individuals over time by their employer.

Date of first annuity benefit payment. — There are two options for the start of benefit payments. The first is an immediate annuity which is only available if a limp sum premium payment is made. Under this plan the first benefit payment is made at the end of the first benefit period following purchase of the annuity. The income benefit period can be monthly, quarterly, semi-annually or annually.

The second is a deferred annuity where the first benefit payment occurs at a stated time at least one year after the annuity is purchased. This can be a calendar date or at a specific age sometime in the future.

Duration of benefit payments. — Another way to classify annuities is by the period of time benefits are paid. The first is the life annuity which provides benefits from a specified date for the remainder of the annuitant's life. This can be either an immediate annuity or a deferred annuity. However once the annuitant dies the balance of the premiums paid in remain with the insurance company. There is no death benefit.

The second approach is the annuity certain which pays benefits from a stated beginning date for a specified period of time. If the annuitant lives beyond the end of the period there are no more benefits. However under the annuity certain if the annuitant dies before the end of the annuity benefit period the remainder is paid to a designated beneficiary.

Number of lives to receive benefits. — Another way that annuities can be classified is by the number lives that are to receive benefits from the annuity. The refund annuity provides an income benefit for the beneficiary if the annuitant dies before the end of stated benefit period (annuity certain).

A no-refund annuity ceases to pay benefits upon the death of the annuitant. The insurance company retains any finds that have yet to be paid under the contract. This applies even to a deferred annuity where no funds have been paid out if it is a no-refund annuity.

By the source of the annuity income. — The annuity can also be classified by the source of its income. The payout benefit units are described by these classifications. A fixed annuity is the conventional form and guarantees that a stated number of dollars will be paid out in benefits on each specific date. The funds behind these annuities have been invested in fixed-dollar investments such as real estate and bonds.

The other form is the variable annuity which pays out based on "units" rather than specific dollar amounts. These units are based on the investment of funds in equity investments such as common stocks. Because equities fluctuate in value so will the units behind the annuity. This approach is based on the concept that during inflationary times the dollar value of the units will increase.

VARIABLE ANNUITIES.

There has been considerable interest in the variable annuity in recent years. This interest was fostered by the fact that inflation can diminish the value of fixed dollar investments. Those who support the variable annuity believe that the annuitant needs financial protection against inflation during the years before the annuity payout. They believe that by using a common stock investment program administered by a life insurance company as the investment vehicle for the annuity this need can be met.

Variable annuities are normally issued on a deferred basis to provide the longer accumulation period that is needed to build the pool of accumulation units upon which the annuity is valued. Annual deposits (premiums) and dividends make up the assets paid into the annuity which become accumulation units. Each month the accumulation units are valued by dividing the market value of the underlying common stock portfolio by the aggregate number of units.

At the time the annuity is to be liquidated the accumulation units are turned into annuity units. The number of annuity units depends on the insurance company's assumptions as to mortality, dividend rates and expenses plus the market value of the assets underlying the annuity units.

The monthly amount paid to the annuitant is determined by multiplying the number of annuity units by the current value of each unit. The higher the market value of the common stocks and the greater the dividends the larger the dollar amount of income for the annuitant.

As the concept of variable annuities has developed many different approaches have been introduced by life insurance companies. Because of this it is important to carefully compare the different plans available.

SPECIAL TYPES OF ANNUITY CONTRACTS.

Because of the existence of several classifications of annuities an annuity contract can be made up of a combination of features. Some of these forms of annuities are:

Temporary annuity. — This form expires when the annuitant dies or at the end of a state period.

Joint life annuity. — This form pays income to two or more annuitants at the same time but ceases when the first dies.

Joint and last survivor annuity. — Under this form income is paid to two or more annuitants at the same time and continues for the survivor when the first dies.

Survivorship or reversionary annuity. — The benefits are paid to the annuitant upon the death of a nominator who has purchased the annuity. In some cases this may be a combination plan where life insurance proceeds paid on the death of the nominator are used to purchase an annuity for the annuitant.

Annuity certain and for life. — Combines an annuity certain with a deferred life annuity. The first pays for a stated period of time and then the deferred life annuity steps in to pay until death if the annuitant is still living.

LONG-TERM CARE INSURANCE.

Long-Term Care insurance was developed to provide benefits that would fund the cost of care in a nursing home or similar facility. The insured pays a premium over a period of time before the need for long-term care arises. This is much like an annuity where funds are paid in advance for a future need.

There is no standard policy but the major features are 1) the Benefit period, 2) the Daily benefit and 3) the Elimination period. An insured qualifies for the benefit by meeting policy requirement such as being unable to perform some activities of daily living, medical necessity or cognitive impairment.

The Benefit period, which is the length of time the insurance benefits will be paid, can be for one year to lifetime. The insured selects the benefit period at the time the policy is issued. The Daily benefit is also selected and is set at a maximum amount such as $120 or $180.

Coverage under the policy typically covers skilled nursing home care, intermediate nursing care and custodial care. Some policies also cover home healthcare services. The policies vary as to the types of other services available. It is important to review these features.

An inflation guard feature on policies will provide an automatic increase in the Daily benefit such as 5 percent annually for the next 10 or 20 years. Premiums for these policies are deductible under the federal income tax code.

SOCIAL SECURITY ADMINISTRATION-OLD AGE & SURVIVOR PROGRAM.

Under the Social Security Administration is the Old Age, Survivors, Disability and Health Insurance program (OASDHI) which provides a monthly benefit to eligible individuals upon their reaching the qualifying age and status.

The program is funded by the worker and employer through a taxing mechanism during the working years. The amount of Old Age benefit is based on the funds paid in during the worker's lifetime and other qualifying factors.

The Survivor benefit is base on the primary Old Age benefit and is available to the spouse and children. This continues after the worker's death. There is also a death benefit of $255 which is paid to the survivor.

CHAPTER SEVEN

BASIC PRINCIPLES & CONCEPTS OF HEALTH & DISABILITY INSURANCE

INTRODUCTION.

Health insurance provides economic protection for loss caused by accident or sickness. Because of this health insurance is important for individuals or families. The basic categories of health insurance are Medical Insurance and Disability Insurance.

There are various types of policies available to provide both individual and group insurance coverages in many areas of health insurance. There are also several forms of health insurance providers found in the marketplace.

While there are no standard form of health insurance policies there are certain common provisions that are included in the policies as well as some provisions that are required under state regulation. There are also some federal regulations that apply to health insurance policies.

MEDICAL INSURANCE.

The medical insurance causes of loss (perils) are accident and sickness. The three basic categories of medical insurance are medical expense insurance, dental expense insurance and limited medical policies.

MEDICAL EXPENSE INSURANCE.

Coverage for medical expense insurance is available in individual and group policies. Both forms generally provide similar services. However the policies are modular in form. This means that a particular medical expense policy may have totally different provisions or benefits than another medical expense policy.

Because of this it is generally difficult to compare one medical expense policy to another because the number and provisions of the modules may vary widely. As an example, one policy might cover any and all x-rays. Another policy might cover only $25.00 per x-ray. A third policy might limit the number of x-rays per policy year. Because of this it is important to keep policy characteristics in mind when reviewing policies.

Under group health insurance policies, family offspring are normally covered from birth until they complete college or reach a stated age. Physically incapacitated children may be covered for a longer period of time.

Medical expense insurance policies would be assumed to provide worldwide coverage as they do not define a territory. However, some policies may limit coverage while traveling or living abroad. Policy forms may restrict coverage to particular physicians or hospitals yet have limited exceptions.

There are two benefit levels of medical expense insurance policies. One form provides only the basic medical expense coverages while the other form offers major medical expense coverages.

Basic Medical Expense coverages. — These coverages often have deductibles on an annual per person and per family basis. They may also have internal limits on specific benefits such as a dollar limit on certain tests. The three areas of basic medical expense coverages are 1) Hospital expense, 2) Surgical expense and 3) Miscellaneous Medical expense.

Hospital expense coverage. — This is the coverage for room and board expenses of an insured who is admitted to the hospital. It often listed on the policy as the "average cost of a two-bedded room" in that way the insurance company is not locked in at a certain dollar benefit level. This approach also enables the insurance company to pay different dollar levels of benefit depending on the locale of the policyholder.

Surgical expense coverage. — This section identifies the maximum amount that will be paid for various types of surgeries. It may also be called a surgical schedule. Another approach used for surgical costs is a relative value schedule. In this instance a numerical value or weight is assigned to each surgical procedure and multiplied by a dollar amount. This is an attempt to pay the "reasonable and customary" charges that prevail in the insured's area by adjusting the dollar amount.

Miscellaneous medical expense coverage. — This section covers all other chargeable items that are included in this general policy area. Some items may have a dollar limit or time restriction and may vary depending on the type of item or the location of the policyholder.

Major Medical Expense insurance. This coverage was originally designed as a separate policy form to overlay the basic medical expense policy. Its purpose was to provide a comprehensive high limit excess coverage in addition to the basic policy.

Today the coverage is normally issued as a Comprehensive Major Medical Expense policy. This singular form offers primary coverage with an individual and family annual deductible and a coinsurance contribution by the insured. The policy will be issued with a high dollar limit or even no dollar limit on the individual coverages. However, the policy will generally have a lifetime maximum dollar amount per insured. Medical care may be limited for particular procedures.

Coverage limitations on Medical Expense policies. While the policies are deigned to provide broad medical expense coverage the policies will often include limitations on coverage for maternity, mental illness, and alcohol and drug dependency.

Maternity benefits limitation. — This coverage may not be provided in individual policies except by endorsement. Under group policies federal law requires the coverage. There may be an internal policy limit on the amount of prenatal or postnatal care or charges in connection with normal delivery, surgical delivery, miscarriage or abortion.

Mental illness coverage. — Insurance benefits can be limited as to the total amount payable under the policy, the amount payable per office visit and/ or the number of office visits. A coinsurance provision may apply as well.

Alcohol and drug dependency. — This type of treatment may be restricted to inpatient care and have a limit on the number of days of treatment.

Cost-containment provisions. Various methods of cost containment have been developed by the health care industry and have been added by insurance companies to their policies. These methods are designed to encourage the insured to be more selective in their medical care expenses. These provisions include pre-admission testing, outpatient surgery, hospice care and second surgical opinions.

Pre-admission testing. — Generally these tests are done on an outpatient basis for non-emergency surgery. In emergency situations tests are completed following the admission of the insured.

Outpatient surgery. — This involves surgery which does not require the patient to be hospitalized overnight. In recent years the number and types of outpatient surgery has increased significantly.

Hospice care. — Terminally ill patients often receive hospice care which includes counseling service for the patient and family members. While it can involve the use of medication and life support devices it may not require full hospital services. The benefits are usually available for care provided outside the hospital setting either at home or at a hospice care center.

Second surgical opinions. — When elective surgery is involved the insured may be required to obtain a second or even a third surgical opinion to confirm that the procedure is necessary. If an insured decides to have the surgery without obtaining a second surgical opinion the policy may limit payment by a percentage amount.

Medical Expense exclusions. Policy exclusions found in the policies include many of the following: Intentional injury, Prescription drugs for outpatient use, Dental care except for some emergency care, Eye exams, Cosmetic surgery, Infertility procedures, Treatment not authorized by a physician, Treatment in a government facility and Treatment available under a Workers Compensation Act

LIMITED MEDICAL EXPENSE POLICIES.

These policies provide limited insurance coverage for specific types of losses. Examples are Dread Disease policies (cancer and others), Hospital Income (indemnity), Travel Accident insurance and Credit Disability insurance.

Dread Disease policies. — This type of policy provides limited hospital and miscellaneous medical expenses benefits for cancer, polio and several dread diseases among them such things as meningitis, smallpox and encephalitis. There can be internal limits on one or more of the covered diseases. Benefits are paid in addition to any other health coverage of the insured.

Hospital Indemnity insurance. — The policies pay a stated dollar amount during the period the insured is confined to a hospital. The available benefit is an amount per day, week or month and is paid regardless of any other health insurance. The coverage provides income that can be used to supplement other health insurance during a hospital stay. The benefits may be greater if the insured is in an intensive care unit.

Travel Accident insurance policies. — Benefits are available for accidental death and dismemberment losses incurred while traveling. Some policies may be limited to specific types of travel or transportation while others may provide 24-hour-a-day coverage from any type of travel related accident. Coverage can apply from the time the insured leaves home until returning.

DENTAL EXPENSE INSURANCE.

There are both individual and group dental expense policies available. When the insurance is offered as part of a group insurance plan the benefits can be provided on either a comprehensive basis or a scheduled basis. An individual insurance plan may also offer either type of plan.

Comprehensive plan. — Similar to a comprehensive major-medical expense policy where payment is made on the basis of reasonable and customary charges with a deductible and coinsurance provision applying.

Scheduled plan. — Similar in approach to a surgical expense policy where a maximum amount is stated for various types of services.

Both individual and group policies encourage preventive dental care by providing for routine checkups and cleaning of teeth. The coverage may be subject to an annual limit per covered person with inside limits that apply to items such as dentures, bridges, inlays, crowns and braces. An annual or lifetime per person limit may also apply to some features. The exclusions are similar to those found in major-medical expense policies.

DISABILITY INSURANCE.

Disability insurance policies provide income replacement when the insured is disabled because of accident or sickness. Disability may be defined in several ways and the cause of the disability may also be restricted. The length of time and amount of benefit paid is another condition of these policies. The policies are issued, either individually or on a group basis.

DISABILITY AS A CAUSE OF LOSS.

Disabled can be defined in disability insurance contracts in a number of different ways. These are 1) The inability of the insured to perform the duties of his or her occupation, 2) The inability of the insured to perform the duties of any occupation for which he or she is fit on the basis of experience, education, or training and 3) The inability of the insured to perform any kind of work.

Of these the first definition the "inability to perform one's occupation" is the most liberal from the standpoint of the insured. The second definition requires that for disability payments to be made, the insured cannot be able to do any kind of work for which he is reasonably fit to perform.

For example a dentist is injured and cannot use his hand. Under the first definition coverage would be provided. Under the second definition the insurance company might say he cannot practice dentistry but he can teach dentistry. Therefore no coverage would be allowed.

The third definition is the most restrictive and provides the insurance company with a broad ability to deny coverage since they only have to show the ability to do some kind of work, any kind.

Disability restrictions. — Under some disability policy forms coverage is provided only for total disability while others may provide benefits for partial disability. Again it is the definition in the policy that is the key to coverage.

Under some policies residual disability may be recognized and covered. This is a measure of income loss following disability rather than the inability to perform duties. For example, a professional who can return to work on a part-time basis for a limited period could collect a limited benefit until able to fully perform the job.

Covered causes of disability. — These can differ in policies as well. Disability income policies may limit coverage for disability that results from accidental injury only or from either accidental injury or sickness. There are also policies that provide coverage only for non-occupational accident and sickness. An occupational disability policy also could be issued to provide excess coverage over benefits received from workers compensation.

BENEFITS UNDER DISABILITY INCOME POLICIES.

Policy benefits will provide most but not all of the insured's loss of income. The reason for this reduction is that certain job related expenses would not be incurred during the disability period. Benefits may be tax free and if they were to exceed the insured's pre-income disability they could encourage malingering.

Policies have a waiting period before benefits will be paid and the benefit period will be limited. They are designated as short-term (thirteen weeks to two years) disability policies and long-term (over two years) disability policies. Some disability policies provide lump sum benefits that are payable if the insured has permanent injuries or accidental death occurred.

RIDERS USED ON INDIVIDUAL DISABILITY INCOME POLICIES.

Two types of riders are the cost-of-living rider and the guaranteed purchase option rider. The former increases the benefits based on a cost of living index and the latter allows the insured to increase monthly benefits without having to show evidence of insurability. Both riders would require additional premium.

BUSINESS FORMS OF DISABILITY INSURANCE.

Business uses of disability insurance include those used to protect a related loss of income when the insured is disabled. Professionals and small business owners with business related loss exposures can use these in addition to the insured's disability income coverage.

Business overhead expense insurance. — This coverage pays those business costs that continue during a disability. Expenses that can continue include rent, utilities, administrative costs, salaries and other expenses normal to operating a business or professional practice if the owner becomes disabled. The coverage is based on the average monthly business expenses subject to a waiting period and provides coverage from twelve to eighteen months.

Disability buy-out insurance — Insurance available to partners and owners of closely held corporations to fund buy-sell agreements in the event that one of the partners or owners becomes disabled and is no longer able to participate in the business. The buy-sell agreement would outline the conditions under which the disabled partner would be required to sell his or her share of the business and indicate the availability of the disability buy-out insurance.

CREDIT DISABILITY INSURANCE.

Similar in purpose to Credit Life Insurance the coverage is designed to provide payment of a debt when the insured is disabled. It can be written either on an individual or group basis with restrictions and limitations on benefits both in amount and in time payable. A waiting period may also be included.

Generally it is a group contract connected with an installment payment plan. The seller holds the policy and the buyer is given a certificate. The policy provides that the installment plan payment will be paid while the insured is unable to do so because of accident or sickness. The contract terms and conditions can vary among different insurance companies. It is often sold along with credit life insurance to protect the creditor in the event of death or disability of the insured.

SOCIAL SECURITY ADMINISTRATION — HEALTH & DISABILITY PROGRAMS.

The primary health and disability program under the Federal government is in the Old Age, Survivors, Disability and Health Insurance program (OASDHI) which is under the control of the Social Security Administration.

Disability benefits — Under Social Security to qualify the employee seeking benefits must have a required number of credits to qualify. Depending on the individual's age at the time of disability the number of credits ranges from twenty to forty.

There is a waiting period and the disability must be one that would last at least twelve months or be expected to result in death. Benefits are determine by the worker's prior earnings and can also be paid to children, a spouse caring for children or a spouse age 62 or older.

Medicare program — This program has various parts which are all directed toward health care costs. These parts are:

Hospital Insurance (Part A) — This part provides inpatient hospital care, skilled nursing facility care, home health care, hospice care and blood transfusions. There are limitations and restrictions on these benefits.

Supplementary Medical Insurance (Part B) — This is a voluntary program that covers physicians' services, clinical laboratory services, outpatient hospital services, home health care visits, other medical and health care services. There is a monthly premium which is subtracted from the monthly social security benefit payment.

Medicare Advantage Plans (Part C) — These are plans offered by private insurance companies which provide both Part A and Part B coverage. It may offer other coverages such as vision, hearing, dental and/or health and wellness programs. Many include prescription drug coverage (Part D). A premium in addition to the Part B premium is also charged.

The different types of Part C plans are Health Maintenance Organization (HMO), Preferred Provider Organization (PPO), Private Fee-for-Service (PFFS) and Special Needs Plans (SNP). There may be other types of Medicare Advantage Plans available.

Medicare Prescription Drug Coverage (Part D) — This program is offered to everyone with Medicare coverage. There are two programs. The first is to add drug coverage to Original Medicare and the second is obtain drug coverage under a Medicare Advantage plan.

Medical Supplement Policies (MediGap Plans). — As Medicare does not provide coverage for all costs many individuals purchase insurance to fill this gap. Medical Supplement policies are regulated by federal law and there are different programs (A thru J) which provide different benefit levels.

DISCLAIMER

Insurance is regulated by the individual state governments who exercise control over policies, rates, producers and the activities of insurance companies. There are also federal regulations particularly in the Health Insurance field where specific provisions are required to be included in health insurance policies.

Administrative regulations, statutes and judicial decisions from various federal and state jurisdictions can also add to, eliminate or modify insurance contracts and their provisions.

Because of these factors the field of insurance and its products are dynamic and subject to change at any time. Thus it is the suggestion of the author that while the material presented in this book has been carefully checked for accuracy the reader may wish to contact a state insurance department if there is any question on the current status of any policy or provision.

Marshall W. Reavis III, PhD

Insurance Education Publishers, LLC

CPSIA information can be obtained
at www.ICGtesting.com
Printed in the USA
LVHW032149130721
692588LV00006B/903